D1443299

boys' toys

PLUME

Published by Penguin Group

Penguin Group (USA) Inc., 375 Hudson Street, New York, New York 10014, U.S.A.

Penguin Group (Canada), 10 Alcorn Avenue, Toronto, Ontario, Canada M4V 3B2 (a division of Pearson Penguin Canada Inc

Penguin Books Ltd., 80 Strand, London WC2R 0RL, England

Penguin Ireland, 25 St. Stephen's Green, Dublin 2, Ireland (a division of Penguin Books Ltd.)

Penguin Group (Australia), 250 Camberwell Road, Camberwell, Victoria 3124, Australia (a division of Pearson Australia Gro Pty. Ltd.)

Penguin Books India Pvt. Ltd., 11 Community Centre, Panchsheel Park, New Delhi – 110 017, India

Penguin Books (NZ), cnr Airborne and Rosedale Roads, Albany, Auckland 1310, New Zealand (a division of Pearson New Zealand Ltd.)

Penguin Books (South Africa) (Pty.) Ltd., 24 Sturdee Avenue, Rosebank, Johannesburg 2196, South Africa

First published by Plume, a member of Penguin Group (USA) Inc.

First Printing, October 2005

10 9 8 7 6 5 4 3 2 1

Copyright © Quid Publishing, 2005

 REGISTERED TRADEMARK—MARCA REGISTRADA

CIP data is available.
ISBN 0-452-28684-0

Printed in China

Conceived, designed and produced by Quid Publishing
www.quidpublishing.com
Publisher: Nigel Browning
Publishing Manager: Sophie Martin
Art Director: Lindsey Johns
Design and Project Management: Essential Works
Photography: Xavier Young

boys' toys

Jed Novick

A PLUME BOOK

CONTENTS

INTRODUCTION

Talking to my nine-year-old daughter about this book we got into a conversation about what life was like when I was a kid. "There was no Internet?" she asked, wide-eyed.

"Er, no," I replied.

"There was no PS2?"

"No."

"No cellphones? GameBoy? No video games at all?"

"No, no, no."

She paused, hands on hips, a look of pity on her tiny features. "I feel sorry for you," she finally stated sympathetically. "How dull was that?"

It's not too often that I get sympathy from my kids, so I pushed things a bit and threw in, "We only had one TV and that was black and white."

With that she shrugged in a "whatever" way and turned on her heel, returning to her color TV-bearing, Internet-wired bedroom.

Having become intimately acquainted with all of the toys that you'll find in this book, I've come to the not too brilliant realization that the Golden Age of toys is that time when you were young. Which for me was when slot cars (like Scalextric) ruled, when there were stores on main street which sold huge multi-lane tracks and displayed cars that you could go and "drive" for an hour. For my daughter, that Golden Age is going to contain NeoPets and her PS2.

Toys, like record collections, are the photo albums of our youth. They spark memories of a time—and of a life—gone by. Usually that time was a more innocent age when all a kid had to worry about was whether Matt would get ambushed by some unmentionable aliens, or the Lone Ranger and Tonto wouldn't get the better of the bad guys.

Pick any page in this book and, if you're between 35 and 55, I guarantee that you'll be wearing a warm smile of recognition as a flood of memories washes over you. (If you're younger than 35, then you're either an archaeologist or you'll be all like, "I feel sorry for you. How dull was that.")

But this book is not all about memories. Most of the toys that you'll find on these pages you could imagine a kid playing with now. For example, I defy any kid—actually, any person—not to lose an afternoon in the company of the design classics in Chapter 11, or anyone not to get off on anything in the Automobiles section—but maybe I'm a little biased about that one. On the other hand, some toys, particularly those in the Computing chapter, seem to be primarily of historic interest. Of course there are also many toys here that would serve better now as a pension than a plaything.

Some toys are apparently timeless and the line between old and new can be blurred. Star Wars is getting ever more popular. So too, arguably, is Star Trek. Lost In Space had a big movie-led revival. Dr Who (from which the Dalek was the undisputed king of toys) is just about to re-launch. Maybe Johnny West and his pals look a bit past it, and Major Matt Mason, too, but who knows? If Matt got the Hollywood treatment with all the stars and big buck SFX, who's to say he wouldn't be a big toy for the next generation?

And that's the joy of toys. Appeal is universal. It doesn't matter how old something looks, if it appealed to a kid once, it will appeal to a kid again. Appeal is timeless, everything else is packaging.

Jed Novick

CLASSIC ACTION HEROES

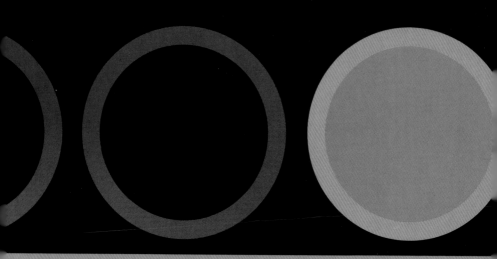

GI JOE

Hasbro
1963–1976

"GI Joe fights for freedom wherever there's trouble."

To his champions, GI Joe is the single greatest brand in the history of boys' toys. He was created in 1963, when a TV show called *The Lieutenant* inspired Don Levine at Hasbro to develop a soldier toy for boys that you could pose. By the next year Levine's designers had developed an 11" soldier with 21 moving parts. Named after the hero of a 1945 William Wellman war film, *The Story of GI Joe*, the toy was an instant success.

Hasbro liked the idea of a "doll" for boys—though no one would ever say that. Joe was an "action figure." He was launched with 75

Joe with facial hair, part of the 1970 Action Team

JOE UPDATE

1976: Mike Power, Atomic Man and Bulletman were introduced. Joe got a radical new muscle body.

1976: The GI was dropped with the launch of an 8" figure called Super Joe.

1982: The Real American Heroes were smaller (like the fashionable Star Wars toys), had exotic names like Snake Eyes and Scarlett, and were promoted in a very successful cartoon series and Marvel comic book. It was a success (except for Eco Force, Drug Elimination Force, and Star Brigade) and some lines ran for 13 years.

1992: Joe is re-introduced under the Hall of Fame series. They were not very poseable, though.

1995: Sgt Savage and his Screaming Eagles and GI Joe Extreme proved to be short-lived.

1996: Hasbro launched the Classic Collection, with Joe sporting a body that looked and felt like the vintage GI Joes. Later that year, Hasbro brought out the classic GI Joe: the Masterpiece Edition.

GI JANE

Of all the GI Joe spin-offs, possibly the most curious was GI Nurse. Released in 1967, it is now so rare that mint-in-box models can fetch up to $6,000 on the collectors' market. Unofficially called GI Jane, she came with a World War II-era nursing uniform, white hose, a small hat bearing a red cross, white shoes, a small medic bag, bandages, crutches, splints, and a bottle of plasma. Which all sounds fine if it wasn't for the sad fact of her appearance. Basically, she looked like Joe in a blonde wig. After a year, Jane was taken off the shelves.

different products relating to the four branches of the military—army, navy, air force and marines—accompanied by a marketing campaign as precise as a military operation. By the end of the 1960s, though, sales of military-themed toys were fading, possibly influenced by the anti-Vietnam War movement. So Hasbro took Joe into space, the oceans, and exotic deserts.

In 1970, the Adventure Team line was launched and off Joe went, fighting wild beasts and nature, recovering mummies and golden idols. More importantly, he now looked more like a male model than a grim-faced fighter. He also had life-like hair and the famous "Kung Fu grip." Sales rocketed again. The Adventure Team line proved more successful than the military-era GI Joe.

Eventually Joe's popularity faded as life (and toys) developed and became more sophisticated. By 1976 production had stopped. Later attempts to re-position Joe in the modern world (see panel) never really worked.

Vintage Joe catalogs detailing various outfits and poses

ACTION MAN

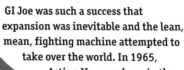

Palitoy/Hasbro
1965–1984

GI Joe was such a success that expansion was inevitable and the lean, mean, fighting machine attempted to take over the world. In 1965, Action Man was born in the UK.

Made by Palitoy under license from Hasbro and named with a nod to the TV show *Danger Man*, he was initially the same as Joe and came packaged the same way, except that there was no UK equivalent of Action Marines.

The figure and head were the same as GI Joe's, while the early versions of Action Man had uniforms that were direct World War II copies. The face had a discreet battle scar, a porcelain-like quality and a distinguished stare that was supposed to be reminiscent of a war memorial.

According to many collectors, the British Action Man was the best of all the GI Joe variants. They were the most detailed, had the most variations and—crucially—Palitoy didn't stop making the 12" model until 1984.

A 1960s Grenadier
Guards uniform

HAIRY GUY

Most of the range's stylistic changes originated with Action Man. One of the most famous was in 1970 when the blond and black flock-haired Action Man were introduced. The original suffered from "hair-rub" where patches of the hair color would rub away to reveal flesh-colored scalp. Plus, the hats and helmets would slip about on his shiny head. (A condition the author is increasingly familiar with.) While the flocked hair might have looked like something you'd use to clean a particularly greasy plate, it did the job. It was strong, didn't wear and didn't rattle.

Bearded heads were introduced soon after in 1971 and a long-sideburned head—nicknamed George after the soccer player George Best—was manufactured in small numbers.

The head was remodeled, became softer and the scar was enhanced. In 1973 improved figures with "gripping hands" were launched.

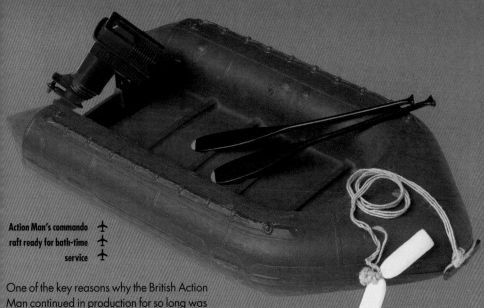

Action Man's commando ✈ ✈
raft ready for bath-time ✈ ✈
service ✈

One of the key reasons why the British Action Man continued in production for so long was that, unlike in the US, there was no significant anti-Vietnam War movement to discredit its military. Therefore, unlike Hasbro, Palitoy was under no pressure to play down the soldier aspects of its hero. Though Action Man's military outfits took on a distinctly British feel—the sets are from the Regimental Series and include such un-American names as the Life Guard, Blues and Royals, 17th/21st Lancers, and the very rare Argyll and Sutherland Highlander—they are still highly collectable. The British model also had a sports line: football, cricket, judo, the Olympics, and so on.

The seventies were a time for re-adjustment, however. In 1976 the legendary "Eagle-Eyes," housed in a slightly larger head and operated by a small lever on the back of the skull, was introduced. Fun as it was, one of the unfortunate by-products of the Eagle-Eyes was his looking permanently astonished. Other models were introduced, including Atomic Man, Tom Stone (a black commando), Bullet Man and the Intruder.

In 1978 a new Muscular Physique was introduced with the tag-line "Bigger Muscles, More Realistic Body," wearing moulded blue trunks and a sun-tan. The original Action Man would have laughed.

Action Man stopped production in January 1984, though like GI Joe, he was brought back in the 1990s for a commemorative series which, though authentic enough and beautifully packaged, never had the heart or soul of the original.

There is an Action Man currently available but only the name remains the same. In every other detail, the new street fighting AM is as far removed from the original as the 21st century is from the 1960s.

CAPTAIN ACTION

Ideal
1966–1968

In Captain Action's first year, Ideal made deals with different comics and created nine different outfits. From DC Comics there was Superman, Batman, and Aquaman, Captain America and Sgt. Fury from Marvel, Flash Gordon, the Phantom, Steve Canyon, and the Lone Ranger (plus Tonto) from newspaper syndicates. Each outfit came with a face mask, a detailed costume, boots, and a handful of accessories.

Superman was a problem, though. In the comic books, he used no gadgetry and had no gimmicks, but here he was given a phantom zone projector, arm and leg shackles, and a chunk of Kryptonite. For those moments when there weren't any emergencies and he just wanted to relax and go for a walk, he came with Krypto, his faithful dog.

It was as inevitable as night following day. Ideal watched, saw, and learned from GI Joe's huge success—and in 1966 launched Captain Action. However, while Joe was limited to the three branches of the military, Captain Action took the idea of interchangeable outfits one step further. Ideal looked at the success of the *Batman* TV show and decided to link Captain Action to any number of comic book heroes.

It was a simple idea: the basic figure wore a blue and black outfit with a colorful "CA" emblem on his chest, and came with a blue ray gun, sword, and hat. Captain Action could be played with on his own, but the real fun (and Ideal's real profits) were to be had with the additional costumes. By slipping a mask over his head and replacing his standard outfit and accessories, you could instantly change him into… Batman! The Flash Gordon outfit had a white space suit and two-

Today, the most collectable outfits belong to the Green Hornet, which was cancelled earlier than the others, possibly due to the cancellation of his TV series in 1967.

In a neat turnaround, in 1968 DC Comics produced a Captain Action comic. Only five issues were made before it was cancelled.

Captain Action as Flash Gordon
✈ ✈ ✈

CITIZENS OF MONGO -- RISE UP TO DEFEAT MING!

SAVE PLANET EARTH !

I HAVE RETURNED, EVIL BEWARE!

LET JUSTICE BE DONE !

INCLUDES:
Captain Action figure,
Atomic Laser pistol,
Lightning blade,
cap and boots.

HERO SERIES

✈
✈
✈ **The original Captain Action
outfit revived**

piece helmet, blue space belt, silver ray gun, and a two-piece guidance gun. The second series of CA costumes all included a silver video-matic flasher ring. Each ring had a picture of its own character on it. But when you changed the angle… it magically changed into Captain Action.

Captain Action's vehicle was the 21" amphibian Silver Streak which came with removable engine cover, two working rocket launchers, and rockets.

DR EVIL

In 1967, Captain Action was given an adversary, a "fiend from outer space"—Dr Evil. He was dressed in a blue tunic, gold pendant, sandals, and came equipped with a laser gun and human face mask. But his most noticeable characteristics were his light blue skin and exposed brain. In 1968, shortly before Captain Action was cancelled, Dr Evil was given a special Gift Set, known as The Lab Set, which included the basic figure, but also a lab coat, two new disguises, several new weapons and a "hypnotic eye." Who said crime doesn't pay?

JOHNNY WEST

Louis Marx Toy Co.
1965–1976

Johnny goes for
his gu

So much starts with GI Joe. As the 1950s drew to a close, Louis Marx & Co. of the US was one of the biggest toy manufacturers in the world. They decided to use their state-of-the-art plastic injection technology, which moulded the figure's clothes to his body, to create a similar 12" articulated figure: Stony Smith, the Paratrooper. Poor Stony fell on hard ground,though. Marx's next attempt was a fully-clothed figure called The All-American Fighter, a.k.a. "Buddy Charlie." He was available as a marine, pilot, sailor, or soldier.

Then as Ideal went after comic books to secure Captain Action's market (see page 14), so Marx went after the still hugely popular TV western shows such as *Gunsmoke*, *Bonanza* and *The Virginian* in 1965, and produced Johnny West, a 12" cowboy action figure, reputedly named to honor John Wayne.

Johnny West was hugely popular and is the toy now most associated with the Marx name. Launched in 1966, the Fort Apache Fighters line (see following pages) consolidated the name. But times change as do boys' toys and in1972, Marx sold out to Quaker Oats. In 1975 the company launched the Johnny West Adventure Series (a.k.a. JWA series) and JW was given a new lease of life, but despite the proliferation of accessories and toys JW was about to go the way of John Wayne himself. Boys now wanted spacemen, not cowboys.

JED GIBSON

Today, the most sought after figure is Jed Gibson in the Johnny West Adventure line. The first and only black model made by Marx (in 1975), he was a cavalry scout, and is now quite hard to find.

CHIEF CHEROKEE

Louis Marx Toy Co.
1965–1976

Chief Cherokee was launched in 1965, shortly after JW. Not to be messed with, The Chief was an uncompromising figure. The same year also saw Thunderbolt, a western range horse that both Johnny and the Chief could ride, introduced. Would it bring the old adversaries together? Or give them something new to fight about?

The Chief looks unamused

The Chief wasn't the only Indian that JW faced. There was also Fighting Eagle and Geronimo although, as with all toy companies, little attention was paid to facts in creating the doll based on the American Indian's greatest warriors. Geronimo was an Apache and fought the cavalry, not the 7th Cavalry unit Marx produced. Fighting Eagle was an Iroquois from the East coast around New York and not the Wild West. The most stylish villain, though, was Sam Cobra. He dressed head-to-toe in black and had a goatee beard.

KNIGHT TIME

Related—but not by blood—was the Marx Noble Knights and Vikings series. Launched in 1968 but gone by 1973, it included Sir Gordon the Gold Knight, Sir Stuart the Silver Knight, Odin the Viking Chieftain and Erik the Viking, complete with horses for all. For collectors today, the hardest to find is the British Sir Cedric the Black Knight. What Chief Cherokee would have made of it all... who knows?

Chief **CHEROKEE**
the *movable* **INDIAN** *by* MARX

#2063

Fully Jointed CONSTRUCTION!
...YOU CAN BEND HIS ARMS WRISTS · KNEES LEGS AND TURN HIS HEAD...

HE WILL STAND · SIT KNEEL · RIDE A HORSE!

Completely **OUTFITTED** with his own **TRAPPINGS AND WEAPONS**

☆ PUT HIM IN **1001** DIFFERENT POSITIONS!

OVER 11 inches **TALL** OF SOLID POLY-PLASTIC

MARX

CAPT TOM MADDOX

Louis Marx Toy Co.
1966–1975

THERE'S ALSO

A quick run-through of Capt Maddox's accessories shows how detailed Marx sets were: Saber (Union type, black), Blanket Roll (black), Pistol (New Army Revolver, black), Bugle (cavalry type, black), Canteen (cavalry type, US on side, black), Binocular (black), Rifle (1873 Springfield, black), Folded Gloves (yellow), Bandana (yellow), Binocular case (black), Binocular case strap (black), Pistol belt (black), Kepi (black), Scout Hat, upturned brim (black), Officers Hat (black), Rifle strap (black), Spur straps (black), Spurs-back (part-black), Map Case (black), Map Case Strap (black), Two stick-on epaulets.

Buoyed by the success of Johnny and the Chief, Marx branched out into the Fort Apache Fighter Series. Again similar to popular TV shows—this time primarily the smash-hit *F-Troop*—the FAF was more Cavalry than cowboy. The most popular figure of the series was Capt Maddox. A blue figure with black hair, Maddox was strong and upright, his own man.

Other figures included Bill Buck, Geronimo, Fighting Eagle, Zeb Zachary and General Custer. Other playsets added included a cardboard full-scaled Fort Apache for the 12" figures. In 1974 Marx brought out another western series: The Best of The West series. The main addition was the female Indian figure "Princess Wildflower"—a precursor to Disney's Pocahontas and a sure sign that the political climate was changing. Having a sympathetic Indian who was a little more than a target was one thing. Having a sexy Indian Princess was something else entirely.

But the "something else" wasn't good. The change in the climate meant that the writing was on the wall for Johnny West and the whole of the West-world. Times had changed—the romance of the Western era was long gone and in 1975, Marx decided to discontinue the series.

ELECTROMAN

You had to feel sorry for Electroman. You couldn't help but wonder if he'd have done better if he'd just stayed at home. It's ironic, but the company that made him was called Ideal. He was too big— 16" tall—wore a less-than-stylish red and yellow costume, and had only one enemy—Zogg The Terrible—whose name had already been used on another line.

Electroman, who ran from 1977–1978, carried light beams in his head that had three functions: guard, radar and stun. Zogg The Terrible also had the same facility.

There was an unrelated doll launched in 1977—Ideal's black Magic Hair Crissy—which also wore the same outfit. Maybe it was the costume that was cursed. Crissy didn't last long, either.

Commander Chuck welcomes you

Made between 1969–1970, the Sea Devils were Mattel's aquatic version of the successful Major Matt Mason line (see page 50).

There are two basic Devils—Commander Chuck Carter (orange wetsuit) and Rick Riley (black wetsuit)—and each came with a battery of accessories: oxygen tanks, fins, hoses, face mask, helmet, battery-powered sea sled and a powered pump which helped them to dive and resurface. They have Kretar and his shark Zark for enemies, the latter with a wound up tail that would swish back and forth to propel him through the water. The largest of the Sea Devil sets had an amphibious car (pictured).

MARVEL COMIC SUPERHEROES

Mego
1971–1982

With the growth of popularity of action heroes it was inevitable that the toy manufacturers would seek to extend the range. The most prolific company at the beginning of the 1970s was Mego, which had cleverly secured the rights to comic heroes and morning TV names.

Mego launched its Comic Action Hero series in 1971 with an Action Jackson figure, quickly followed by Batman & Robin, Superman, and Aquaman. It was the success of this that prompted the popular 8" World's Greatest Super Heroes with the Fantastic Four series in 1972—Mr Fantastic, The Invisible Girl, Thing, The Human Torch. Sadly, there actually was an action figure in The Invisible Girl's box. Mego didn't confine their thoughts to superheroes though: in 1974 they made a Wizard Of Oz set and in 1975 a Waltons set, too.

Produced from 1974 to 1975, the Bend 'n' Flex Heroes range ran alongside the 8" models. They were smaller—5"—and cheaper but curiously charming. The range covered the Superheroes and their respective Arch Enemies, from Batman's The Joker to Superman's Mr Mxyzptlk (and try saying that when you're in a telephone booth).

In 1979, the Pocket Heroes series was released. The bodies were the same as thosae of the Comic Action series, but had straight legs and arms, and the figures included Batman, Robin, Superman, Spiderman, the Hulk, Green Goblin, Wonder Woman, Aquaman and Captain America. Disappointingly for

ALTER EGOS

The rarest and most sought-after Mego sets are the Alter Egos. They were sold exclusively in 1974 through the Montgomery Ward's catalog. There were four Alter Egos—Clark Kent, Peter Parker, Bruce Wayne and Dick Grayson—and all came dressed in their civilian outfits but—cleverly—in colors that reflected their superhero identities. Thus Peter Parker's outfit was red jumper and blue slacks. The rarest Alter Ego of all is Bruce Wayne/Dick Grayson which came in a twin set. Alter Egos are so sought after that a fake Clark Kent was recently offered on Ebay. It was withdrawn very quickly.

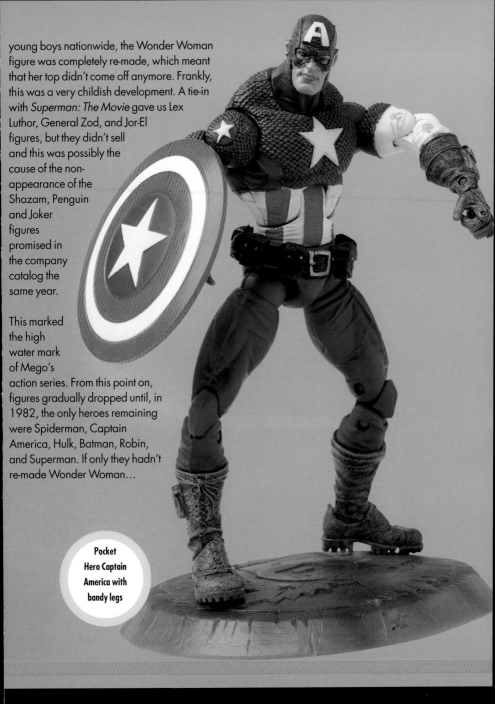

young boys nationwide, the Wonder Woman figure was completely re-made, which meant that her top didn't come off anymore. Frankly, this was a very childish development. A tie-in with *Superman: The Movie* gave us Lex Luthor, General Zod, and Jor-El figures, but they didn't sell and this was possibly the cause of the non-appearance of the Shazam, Penguin and Joker figures promised in the company catalog the same year.

This marked the high water mark of Mego's action series. From this point on, figures gradually dropped until, in 1982, the only heroes remaining were Spiderman, Captain America, Hulk, Batman, Robin, and Superman. If only they hadn't re-made Wonder Woman…

Pocket Hero Captain America with bandy legs

TV & FILM

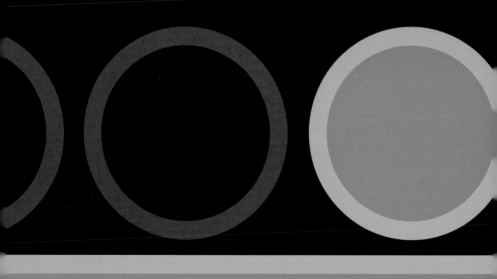

JAMES BOND

Gilbert, Corgi, Mego
1965–Present day

BOND TRADING

Some Bond memorabilia is worth huge amounts now. For Bond collectors, one of the most sought-after items is the 1965 attaché case from Gilbert/Multiple Products (1965). In good condition, these can fetch up to $2,000.

Another Gilbert item, the 1965 battery-operated Aston Martin, is worth over $500. It did everything the more famous Corgi model did—including the bullet-proof shield to the machine guns—except that it did it itself.

The Bond villain Jaws—not a shark but able to bite

While the first James Bond film, *Dr No*, was released in 1962, it wasn't until *Thunderball* came out in 1965 that toy makers really took notice.

A.C.Gilbert was first out of the blocks in 1964 with a range of 3¼″ plastic figures: Bond (in black business suit with cap-firing pistol), Dr No, Oddjob, Domino, Largo, M, Miss Moneypenny and Goldfinger. A year later came *Thunderball* and various new toys. Bond came with a scuba suit. Bond and Oddjob also came as 11″ figures. Oddjob was possibly the best of all the dolls—"Throws Deadly Derby!" "Delivers Swift Karate Blow!" proclaimed the box. His arms were spring operated so

The Lotus came with a cardboard sea

✈ ✈ ✈

A young kid—not a little unlike your author—had a special car when he was a small boy. It was a James Bond Aston Martin DB5 from either *Goldfinger* (1964) or *Thunderball* (1965)—the same car was used in both. It was a Corgi, gold with a red interior. A gun shield came up from the boot, machine guns hid behind the headlamps. The sun roof opened but you'd have to be careful because the ejector seat was lethal. It was, as it said on the box, "Authentic!" Where it is now, I don't know. But recently there was one on auction for $695.

The Lotus Esprit that worked in water

that he threw his hat—which happily was not blade-rimmed like the real thing. When Oddjob's left arm was released it chopped down. Gilbert also made a battery-operated Aston Martin in 1965 that did everything the more famous Corgi version did—from employing the bullet-proof shield to the machine guns projecting from the front.

In 1979, Mego released a series of Moonraker dolls that were mainly "adapted" from other Mego figures. MicroMachines produced models from *Goldfinger*, *The Spy Who Loved Me*, and *Moonraker*.

A British company, Lone Star, also made a range from the later *Goldeneye* period. But it is the sheer diversity of the Bond toys available that's striking. From Milton Bradley's card game to a *Goldfinger* jigsaw puzzle to a model of Dr No's dragon tank… if there was something associated with James Bond, you could probably get it for Christmas.

THE SIX MILLION DOLLAR MAN

Kenner Toys
1974–1978

In March 1973 we first heard the immortal words, "Gentleman, we can rebuild him, we have the technology." Steve Austin, human pilot, was turned into The Bionic Man, half-man, half-machine, for $6 million.

Based on Martin Caidin's novel *Cyborg*, ABC's series made a huge star out of Lee Majors. In 1974 Kenner Toys created The Six Million Dollar Man action figure. He was just over a foot tall, had a see-through Bionic eye which made everything look far away and realistic skin that rolled up on his Bionic arm to reveal his circuitry. There was a switch on his back that, when his head was turned to the right, allowed him to lift up heavy objects with his bionic arm.

Kenner produced 14 different outfits and Bionic adventure packs for The Six Million Dollar Man, and in 1977 changed Steve's arm to include the Bionic Grip, which looked the same but was metallic.

Steve, dressed for action. Or Yoga.

BIONIC BABE

What's good for the TV hero is good for the action hero and Jamie Sommers, The Bionic Woman (played by Lindsay Wagner), got not only her own series but her own model. You too could re-create the horrific sky-diving accident which left Jamie a wreck. You too could re-build her.

STARSKY AND HUTCH

MEGO
1976–1983

FOR GROWN-UP BOYS

The ultimate Starsky and Hutch boys' toy—maybe the ultimate of all boys' toys—was the car. Not a picture of the car, not a model of the car, but the big, moving, wheel-spinning car itself. In 1976, the final year of production, the Ford Motor Company made 1,000 Starsky and Hutch cars. Proper Gran Torinos with the stripe and all the trimmings.

On September 3, 1975, on ABC's *Wednesday Night At The Movies* season, a pilot for a new kind of cop show hit the screens. *Starsky and Hutch* was quite unlike anything that had been seen before.

It came complete with the iconic car of the decade: Starsky's 1975 Ford Gran Torino. The most instantly recognizable vehicle of its day, it was perfect for toy manufacturers. Johnny Lightning, Corgi and Scalextric all made models. Mego's 15" long "Spin-Out" car ($12.97) was typical. It had "Twist Out" action—when it hit an object it changed direction. The lights blinked, sirens sounded and it came complete with a lamp post and a couple of rubbish bins, all the better for knocking over during a street chase. You could buy 8" Starsky and Hutch figures for $3.94 each. The car is now worth up to $300, the same as a good condition Corgi Gran Torino.

A better actor than Huggy Bear? ✈ ✈ ✈

The show ended on August 21, 1979, but the toys kept on coming.

THE LONE RANGER

Gabriel/Hubley 1973

"Hi ho, Silver—away!" is as familiar a cry as "Up, up and away" or "To infinity and beyond." Ever since the Lone Ranger first entered the nation's consciousness on the radio in 1933 (and TV in 1948), his toys have been produced. But it wasn't until 1973 when Gabriel (through Hubley) made The Lone Ranger Rides Again! line of action figures, that Lone went big time. The Gabriel/Hubley line was sold in America, and later Marx took it overseas.

The Gabriel toy line consisted of six 9" fully articulated action figures (Lone Ranger, Tonto, Butch Cavendish, Red Sleeves, Dan Reid, and Little Bear), four horses (Silver, Scout, Smoke, and Banjo), plus accessories like the Prairie Wagon (below) and a series of adventure sets (including Landslide Adventure, Hidden Rattler Adventure, Apache Buffalo Hunt, Tribal Powwow, Missing Mountain climber, and Red River Floodwaters). Marx added two more figures (El Lobo and Tex Dawson), and nine other sets, including the Mysterious Prospector set. These two Marx figures are the hardest to find (and most expensive), now, fetching over $100 each.

"Someone stole Silver, Kimo-Sabi."

✦✦✦

INCREDIBLE HULK

Mego
1975–1985

CBS's hugely popular TV series ran from March 1978 to June 1982, but Mego pre-empted TV by releasing a Hulk figure as part of its Super Heroes set in 1975. The Mego Hulk might have disappointed some of the angry green giant's fans though, because for some reason Mego made him 8" tall— smaller than many of his contemporaries. It's a curious thing that the Hulk's original box— and bear in mind the Hulk's character here—was pink.

So what you had was a diminutive Hulk in a pink box. No wonder it didn't sell at first. But the Hulk turned into Mego's late bloomer and what was a modest seller at first, when the TV series aired, became part of Mego's Big Four Superheroes and sales took off.

GERRY ANDERSON: UFO

British born Gerry Anderson's first television show was a children's puppet series called *The Adventures Of Twizzle*. It was so successful that he decided to go into puppetry full-time.

In the early 1960s he produced *Supercar*, a futuristic show which pioneered Super-Marionation, a sophisticated puppetry technique. It was hugely popular in the UK and was sold to America. Despite it's success, *Supercar* didn't generate many spin-off toy products. Remco made a moulded plastic model (1963) in a fetching bright orange, but it wasn't until *Fireball XL5*, Anderson's third marionette series, that merchandise really came into its own. In 1964, Multiple Products Corporation (MPC) produced a large Fireball XL5 spacecraft.

By the time the TV series *UFO* was shown in September 1972 in America, all kids TV shows had tie-in merchandising. This was the first "real people" Gerry Anderson show though, and it confused networks and audiences, running for only one season.

Dinky was the main supplier of *UFO* products and, like all the Gerry Anderson shows, the *UFO* was immaculately conceived. It had futuristic cars, space vehicles and strange-looking people in purple wigs. Inevitably, the most popular items have been the kits and die-cast models of the various vehicles and bases. In 2004 an original Dinky version of Commander Ed Straker's car—gold plate with a blue interior—sold for $200.

The Moonbase was actually bigger...

UFO BOARD?

There was a UFO board game called Red Alert, which could be played in the dark as it had a glow-in-the-dark board and pieces. There was also an American UFO Viewmaster (by GAF) produced in 1969, using photos taken during the filming of the episode "Close Up."

SPACE: 1999

Mattel
1975–1976

DID YOU KNOW ...

In the UK, Palitoy made five figures in 1975. Mego (their US-based owners) never released these figures in America and they go for upwards of $200 from collectors. They were re-released in 2005 by The Figures Toy Company except for the Koenig figure as Martin Landau refused to give permission.

The TV series *Space: 1999* was conceived when the idea for a second series of *UFO* was abandoned (see left). Made with real people, it had pretensions of being philosophical and sensitive.

There soon were, however, toy figures of the crew, the Moonbase and the Eagle One transporter. The TV outfits weren't the funkiest and you can't really blame Mattel for changing them to brighter colours. Commander Koenig (played by Martin Landau) stayed as he was, but the two other figures, Dr Russell (Barbara Bain) and Prof Bergman (Barry Morse), were orange and brown respectively. Mattel's Moonbase Alpha Playset was made in 1976. It comprised a vinyl command center with a light-up Starflash Computer and chairs for the figures. Mattel's Eagle One, also made in 1976, was 2½ ' long, and came with 3" versions of Koenig, Russell, and Bergman. The original price was $14.95.

Dinky also made a series of Eagle transporters and "Pods" that fitted inside them. There was not an original all-white Eagle One.

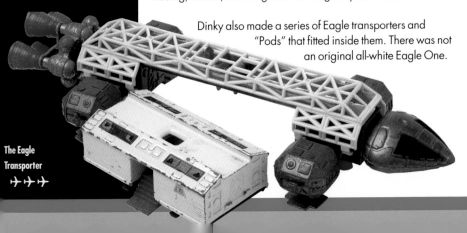

The Eagle Transporter
✈ ✈ ✈

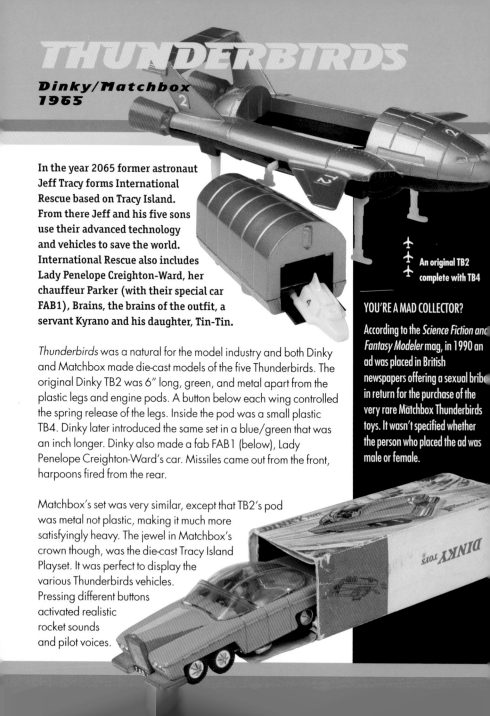

THUNDERBIRDS

Dinky/Matchbox 1965

In the year 2065 former astronaut Jeff Tracy forms International Rescue based on Tracy Island. From there Jeff and his five sons use their advanced technology and vehicles to save the world. International Rescue also includes Lady Penelope Creighton-Ward, her chauffeur Parker (with their special car FAB1), Brains, the brains of the outfit, a servant Kyrano and his daughter, Tin-Tin.

Thunderbirds was a natural for the model industry and both Dinky and Matchbox made die-cast models of the five Thunderbirds. The original Dinky TB2 was 6" long, green, and metal apart from the plastic legs and engine pods. A button below each wing controlled the spring release of the legs. Inside the pod was a small plastic TB4. Dinky later introduced the same set in a blue/green that was an inch longer. Dinky also made a fab FAB1 (below), Lady Penelope Creighton-Ward's car. Missiles came out from the front, harpoons fired from the rear.

Matchbox's set was very similar, except that TB2's pod was metal not plastic, making it much more satisfyingly heavy. The jewel in Matchbox's crown though, was the die-cast Tracy Island Playset. It was perfect to display the various Thunderbirds vehicles. Pressing different buttons activated realistic rocket sounds and pilot voices.

An original TB2 complete with TB4

YOU'RE A MAD COLLECTOR?

According to the *Science Fiction and Fantasy Modeler* mag, in 1990 an ad was placed in British newspapers offering a sexual bribe in return for the purchase of the very rare Matchbox Thunderbirds toys. It wasn't specified whether the person who placed the ad was male or female.

CAPTAIN SCARLET

Dinky
1967–1993

COME BACK SCARLET

With a new CGI animation technique released in 2005, Captain Scarlet is making something of a comeback—well, he is indestructible. Suitably, the Japanese company Bandai announced the launch of a new range of 5" figures of all the Spectrum agents, plus Captain Black and the Angels.

The first of the 32 episodes of *Captain Scarlet* aired on September 29, 1967, and took Anderson's Super-Marionation puppetry method onto a new level. The puppets were more realistic, and the show was darker in tone than anything before.

Captain Scarlet was indestructible—so you could do whatever you wanted with him. His enemies weren't anything more tangible than a couple of lights moving across the ground. Which probably pleased parents more than the marketing department. Typically for an Anderson show, there are now a lot of collectable toys. Apart from the two main characters—Scarlet and Captain Black—there is also the usual paraphernalia of space stations and vehicles.

While *Thunderbirds* may be the most famous Gerry Anderson show, prices of vintage Captain Scarlet memorabilia don't reflect that. A rare large plastic model of Scarlet's SPV (Spectrum Pursuit Vehicle) made by Rosenthal/Century 21 Toys sold for $931 in 2004. A mint copy of Dinky's die-cast model of Scarlet's SPV in its original box and packaging is worth about $300. Even more recent merchandise is gaining in value. A 1993 Angel Interceptor plane (Vivid Imaginations Company) was valued at $50.

TV & FILM   33

STAR WARS

Luke's
speeder bike

Toys come and toys go, pushed and persuaded by the vagaries of fashion and the determination of the marketing boys. This year's "Must Have" is next year's yard-sale product. It's the evolution of life, the Darwinism of the toy department. But every so often, something comes along and kicks that familiar certainty into touch. In May 1977, a film called *Star Wars* opened.

Before we go any further, consider this. Between 1977 and 1984, the two main Star Wars suppliers, Kenner and MPC, sold three hundred million Star Wars toys. Pick yourself up and we'll carry on with the story.

Kenner had been founded in 1947 by brothers Al, Phil and Joe Steiner. They named their company after Kenner Street, in Cincinnati. They immediately had a success with Bubble Matic, but hit pay dirt in 1955 with the phenomenon that was Play-Doh.

FEEL THE FORCE

That first Christmas, demand for *Star Wars* toys proved so high that Kenner couldn't keep up. So they came up with an idea so brilliant you can only admire it. They decided to issue *Star Wars* toy vouchers. You could buy a voucher for the toy and when the toy came in you could redeem the voucher for it. The idea was brilliant. They were, in effect, selling toys that didn't exist.

LET MEGO TOO!

Another company, Mego, had been offered the rights to *Star Wars*. Mego had made a success of 8" action figures (see page 20) called the Comic Action Hero series. In 1977, Mego was offered rights to the (then) little known *Star Wars*. While Mego was considering the situation, Kenner got the rights. Soon Mego realized its mistake and tried to join in, introducing figures in both the 3¾" scale and the 12" size. It didn't help, though. Mego went belly up in 1982.

An X-wing fighter ready for action

In 1967, the company was taken over by General Mills and in 1977, the company acquired the license to sell *Star Wars* merchandise.

The Kenner line of action figures was the most common toy, and the cornerstone of many a contemporary collection. During this period, there were over a hundred figures produced both on card and in blister packs. When first produced, these small figures—plastic, fully poseable and between 2¼ and 4½"—cost between $3.66 and $4.88 for a set of (typically) three.

The first carded *Star Wars* action figure was the four-figure Early Bird kit of late 1977 (Luke Skywalker, R2-D2, Princess Leia, and Chewbacca) but most collectors start with the next set, the first appearance of *Star Wars* figures on individual cards, known to aficionados as "The 12 Backs."

Less well regarded were the 12" figures, such as the R2-D2 (with its "hidden" rear storage compartment for plastic "data tapes"). Sweetly, in the 12" set R2-D2 was about 6" tall. Kenner also made a line of small-scale die-cast metal vehicles, including the Millennium Falcon, Luke's land speeder, both standard and Darth Vader TIE fighters, an X-Wing, a Y-Wing, and an Imperial Star Destroyer.

STAR TREK

Star Trek didn't take off in the toy market in the same way as *Lost In Space* had. The reason was that the early audience was primarily older teens and adults—it was a market that preferred collecting rather than playing.

It was only later, spurred on by the success of both *Star Wars* and the *Star Trek* films, that Trekky merchandising really took off. Mego acquired a *Star Trek* license in 1975—bought from Paramount for a reputed $5,000 advance—and despite early misgivings, their first line proved an immediate success. The initial run included Kirk, Spock, McCoy, Scott and the Klingon. Uhura was soon added.

Mego also produced various playsets—typically with a spinning Transporter Room—and games, such as the Super Phaser II Target Game (1976).

Seems illogical, but Spock was quite popular

In the 1990s, Playmates produced a range of classic Trek toys. There was a range of 5" figures of all the main characters, from Kirk in various guises to bit players such as Harry Mudd, a Star Trek Classic Tricorder, a fully fitted-out Bridge, Dr McCoy's Medical Kit, a phaser, a wrist communicator and a flip-top communicator.

DID YOU KNOW...

In 1996, Mattel made a *Star Trek* Barbie—a blond with a ready smile and a tri-quarter. Just Kirk's type. Just as well, then, that they made a Kirk too.

BUCK ROGERS

HAVE A TWIKI

Probably the best *Buck Rogers* toy—a radio-controlled Twiki—never actually made it past the planning stage. The following is taken from a 1980 toy fair catalog: "A full 12" high Twiki walks forward while turning its head from side to side. It also follows your commands to turn left and right. But that's just the beginning. The radio-controlled transmitter sends your voice through Twiki and makes him beep. In addition, Twiki carries Dr Theopolis, its own LED-lit computer, right on its chest. Twiki, the robot that does so much it's almost human." Sounds cool, huh? Shame it never happened.

NBC's *Buck Rogers in the 25th Century* ran from September 1979 to April 1981. The narrator in the TV series was William Conrad, better known as TV detective Frank Cannon.

Most of the action figures were made by Mego, who produced two lines—3¾" figures and the less-common 12" figures. They covered the range of characters, from Buck himself to the Tiger Man and Twiki. Mego also made play sets and ships including the Marauder and Buck's Starfighter. The rarest vehicle is a Land Rover that only appeared in the series pilot. Mego also made a vehicle that never actually appeared in the show: the Laserscope Fighter.

Typically, Corgi made die-cast miniatures such as the Starfighter, while Milton Bradley produced a board game.

Buck Rogers in his box

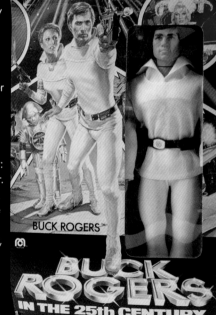

BUCK ROGERS™

BUCK ROGERS IN THE 25th CENTURY

DR WHO AND THE DALEKS

BBC and Corgi
1965–Present Day

Dr Who first hit UK TV screens on November 23, 1963, and is still going strong. There have been long periods when the doctor has not been on our screens but it's probably fair to say that the fan-base has never gone away, nor diminished. There have (so far) been seven Doctors, countless assistants and villains, but whether you're talking about the TV show, the films or the spin-off merchandise, one character dominates— the Dalek.

Designed by Raymond Cusick— not, as often thought, Ridley Scott, who was a BBC staff designer at the time—the Daleks, a heavily armored race of mutants from the planet Skaro, first appeared on the second episode of *Dr Who*. They made an immediate impression, and despite being killed off in that first showing, had to be brought back.

They were simple and easy to make as toys and so, from robots that said "Exterminate, Exterminate" endlessly to packets of breakfast cereal emblazoned with their image, the Daleks were everywhere. Corgi made a range of 3" Daleks in both silver and red that sold particularly well.

A wind-up Dalek. Scary, huh?

Lost In Space—the Swiss family Robinson in space—was one of the classic series of the 1960s. It was the first great space TV show, predating *Star Trek,* and set the toy tie-in agenda.

A *Lost In Space* module

AURORA

The most valuable *Lost in Space* toys today are probably Aurora model kits. The kit featuring the cyclops from the episode "There Were Giants on the Earth" can fetch up to $1,000 in mint condition. (Curiously, the kit neglected to feature Penny Robinson and, though she was a bit girly, this still seems harsh).

The battery-powered motorized Remco *Lost in Space* robot (serial number 760) was 12" tall, with blinking lights and manually movable spring-controlled arms. It was produced in several color combinations, most involving black, though the most popular was red/blue.

Remco's *Lost in Space* Helmet & Gun Set boasted a blue plastic helmet with a clear plastic dome, plus a flashing blue light and a *Lost in Space* logo.

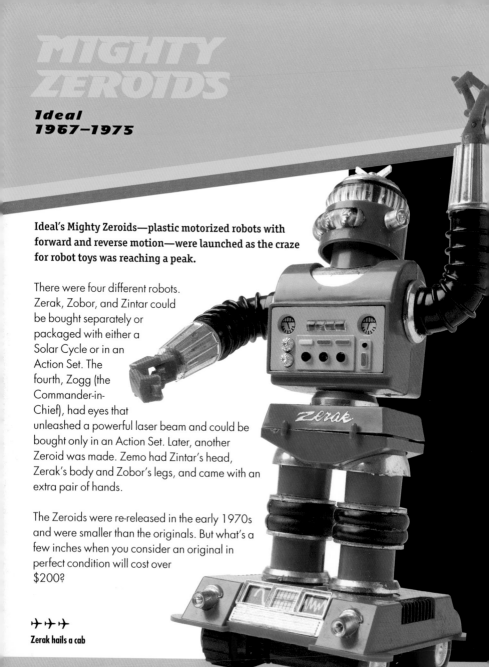

MIGHTY ZEROIDS

Ideal
1967–1975

Ideal's Mighty Zeroids—plastic motorized robots with forward and reverse motion—were launched as the craze for robot toys was reaching a peak.

There were four different robots. Zerak, Zobor, and Zintar could be bought separately or packaged with either a Solar Cycle or in an Action Set. The fourth, Zogg (the Commander-in-Chief), had eyes that unleashed a powerful laser beam and could be bought only in an Action Set. Later, another Zeroid was made. Zemo had Zintar's head, Zerak's body and Zobor's legs, and came with an extra pair of hands.

The Zeroids were re-released in the early 1970s and were smaller than the originals. But what's a few inches when you consider an original in perfect condition will cost over $200?

✈ ✈ ✈
Zerak hails a cab

ROBBY THE ROBOT

Nomura
1955–1960

A black
Nomura
Robby Robot
✈ ✈ ✈

Directed by Fred M. Wilcox and starring Leslie Nielsen, Walter Pidgeon and Anne Francis, *The Forbidden Planet* (1956) is one of the classic science fiction films of all time. Based on Shakespeare's *The Tempest*, it was innovative and thoughtful.

It also marked a milestone in marketing, that revolved around Robby the Robot. The inspiration of every TV and film robot that followed, Robby was designed by Robert Kinoshita and was one of the most elaborate robots created for a film. Built at a cost of $125,000, he used more than 2,600 feet of electrical wiring to operate all the flashing lights, spinning antennae and gadgets that moved inside his transparent, dome-shaped head. He also had a fully-formed personality.

There were very few genuinely licensed Robby toys, but one of the best was the Mechanized Robot made by Nomura in 1955—the year before the film came out. When it was first produced, it was silver but then the film came out with a black robot and, curiously, it changed color. (The silver robot is now highly collectable and extremely expensive.) The robot was reproduced in 1991 and again in 1999, both times in a range of colors.

I, ROBOT

Robby continued his career after *Forbidden Planet*. In 1957 he appeared in *The Invisible Boy*, then smartly moved into TV. His credits include *The Thin Man, Lost in Space, The Twilight Zone, The Love Boat, Columbo, Mork and Mindy* and *Clueless*. Finding himself typecast, he unsuccessfully tried romantic comedy.

CONEHEADS

**Yonezawa
1968**

The inspirationally named Conehead is a Japanese superhero who first appeared in the 1950s television show *Shonen Jet*, but he retained his popularity into the late 1980s because of appearances on *Saturday Night Live*.

One of the benefits of Coneheads was that you could use them again and again. Yonezawa used the body, with no modifications, as the basis for the Robby Robot astronaut, and the Robby Robot.

The first Japanese tin robot to be made was a stiff-legged chap called Robot Lilliput (made by Kitahara) who appeared in 1939. (See panel.)

THE FIRST JAPANESE TIN ROBOT...

Lilliput was a simple clockwork chap, orange /yellow with a clock in his chest. The name "Mionseli" (the designer) is stamped on him. In mint condition in his box, he would fetch over $10,000. There is now a Chinese reproduction available, though.

✦ ✦ ✦ Who are you calling conehead?

SMOKING ROBOT

REHAB ROBOT

How did it come about that so many tin robots were made in Japan? Well, according to Darryl the Robotman, after WWII, the US wanted to aid Japan's industrial rehabilitation and so encouraged it to take on low-profit, small-item manufacturing—things from portable radios to small toys. US companies didn't mind. They thought they could import them cheaply and sell them not so cheaply. What the Americans didn't consider was the Japanese determination to rehabilitate itself and soon companies such as Yonezawa and Horikawa had cornered the market.

A smoking robot—
play with it outside ✈ ✈ ✈

There's something inherently nostalgic about post-war robots. They are, in many ways, the antithesis of our video game world, and this particular model perhaps more than most.

This series of pre-dominantly Japanese tin robots were made so that, as well as moving and having flashing lights, they would breathe out smoke (generated from a small motor). One of the earliest was Yoshiya's Chief Smoky in the mid-1950s, who had a plate on his chest calling him Mr Chief. Battery-operated, he had a small tube pointing out of the top of his head which puffed out smoke as he moved.

The most famous smoking robot was made in 1960 by the Japanese company Yonezawa. Designed by Rikizo Miyazawa, he looked just like a classic robot. But every few paces he would stop, make a loud noise, and puff out smoke from his mouth.

Various
1930s—Present day

Toy guns, cap guns, army guns—they've all been hugely popular boys' toys, both in themselves and as part of other toys, like Roy Rogers or GI Joe. The first ray guns were produced as a spin-off from a movie serial. Long before Captain Kirk was even a twinkle in the eye, space had been seen as, if not the final frontier, then at least the next frontier, and as part of the first Buck Rogers craze, ray guns became the thing to have. A mint condition _Buck Rogers in the 25th Century_ Liquid Helium Ray Gun water pistol from the 1930s sold in 2004 for $4,600.

The advantage that ray guns had over "real" guns was that there were no rules: they could look however you wanted them to look, be whatever you wanted them to be. And in the post-WWII years when plastic took off, designs became really interesting. As a rule, Japanese imports tended to be tin-based; American guns, plastic.

POTATO GUN

No relation to Mr Potato Head—though maybe it was something that kids did with the moustachioed spud when they got bored with him. Potato guns were a cross between cap guns and water pistols that used small pieces of potato as "bullets." They were quite sweet and harmless. But... many kids created their own homemade potato guns. These generally were far more effective than the water-pistol size things you could get in the stores. All you needed was a piece of pipe, a lump of spud and some lighter fuel and...

BURP

Launched at the 1955 New York Toy Fair, Mattel's curiously named metal and plastic Burp Gun has two major claims to fame. Not only was it the world's first automatic cap gun, it was also the first product to sponsor a TV show. Sales weren't going as well as Mattel had hoped and so, in an act of near-desperation, the company decided to take 52 weeks of advertising on the new *Mickey Mouse Club* television show. You might think it odd that a children's TV show should be sponsored by a gun. Which it is. But if you made a film about it, you might win an Oscar.

DCMT was a British company set up in the early part of the 20th century that specialized in making die-cast tools and toys. It changed production to the zinc-alloy "mazak" and spent the War years making, among other things, parts for hand grenades.

By 1956, DCMT had become a cross-Atlantic concern and its toy and model products had taken over the business, particularly its subsidiary Lone Star's cap guns. With its connotations of Texas and the Wild West, Lone Star co-opted the Western image, producing not only merchandise but also a magazine. They even went so far as to create a fictional character, Steve Larrabee, as portrayed by Lone Star staff actor Roy Green.

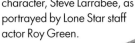

These things are really LOUD

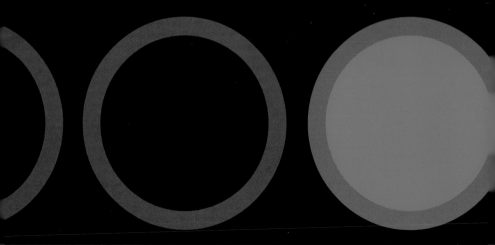

SPACE HEROES

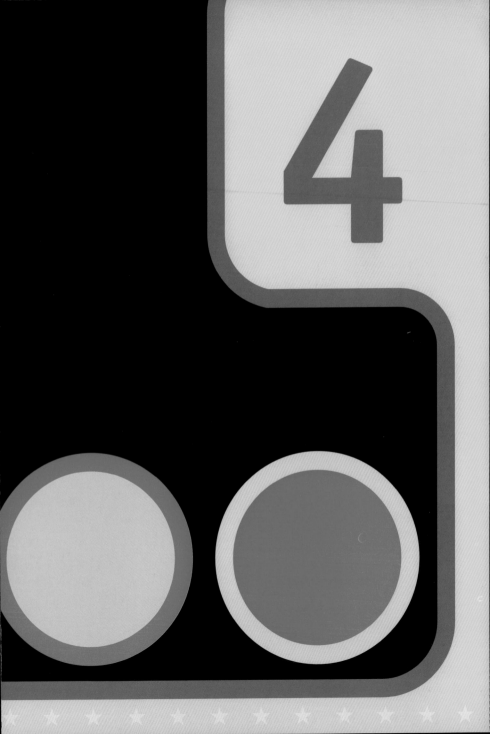

MAJOR MATT MASON

Mattel
1967–1970

While NASA had Neil Armstrong and Buzz Aldrin and the Russians had Yuri Gagarin and untold other cosmonauts all called Boris, Mattel had an astronaut more than able to compete and inspire a generation dreaming of becoming *Gemini* astronauts. Major Mason stood 6" tall and was made during the great period of American space exploration.

Adapted from official space program designs, Major Matt was equipped to deal with anything space could throw at him: violent temperature extremes, radiation, meteorites… it was nothing to Matt. And he wasn't alone. He had two colleagues—Sgt Storm and their great protector from Outer Space, The Amazing Captain Lazer, who had superhuman lazer powers. Together with side-kicks Doug David and Jeff Long they could take on anyone—or anything.

Mason had all the necessary equipment to make lunar exploration possible. The Fireball Space Cannon (space engineered for all Mattel astronauts) moved forward with barrel-blazing beams. Their mighty mobile planet explorer—the AstroTrac—had universal astro-foam traction wheels, perfect for conquering alien terrain. With the Space Station, the inflatable Space Shelter, the Space Crawler and the Satellite Launch Pack there was nothing that Matt wasn't prepared for.

+‹ +‹ +‹

Captain Lazer with ray gun

ODD FACT

In 1978 Mattel re-used the Captain Lazer mould for the figures in its Battlestar Galactica line.

Going where no man had gone before can be a lonely job, so Mattel gave Matt Mason three companions: Sgt Storm (cherry red space suit), Doug Davis (orange yellow space suit) and Jeff Long (first Black astronaut figure).

The Amazing Captain Lazer's eyes lit up and he had a chest emblem and ray gun. He was twice as tall as any other figure. The Firebolt Space Cannon seats Captain Lazer comfortably—or four Matt-sized figures. Mattel later recycled Captain Lazer into the Colonial Warrior from Battlestar Galactica.

Sergeant Storm ready for action

BILLY BLASTOFF— AMERICA'S FIRST BOY IN SPACE

The Eldon Company was best known for its slot cars, but occasionally it branched out into toys—and Billy Blastoff was one of their better known. While Matt Mason was a serious space explorer, Billy was designed to be a kid in space. Physically small (4" high), plastic and baby-faced, Billy was keen and had all the requisite accessories but really you'd worry if he came up against anyone really nasty.

A good condition Billy is hard to find today and a good single figure might cost up to $100 while complete playsets can go for up to $400.

COLORFORMS

The Colorforms Company
1951–Present day

Colorforms is a toy so simple that a child could use it. There's a piece of cardboard and a piece of vinyl. The vinyl is put on the cardboard. And that's it. Uncomplicated and basic.

The Colorforms story began in 1951 when two art students, Harry and Patricia Kislevitz, were looking for materials to use as cheap alternatives to paint. They found a flexible vinyl material and discovered that the vinyl stuck to the semi-gloss paint in their bathroom. Being artists, they cut shapes out of the material and placed them on the walls. Their friends loved it. "They would go in and do the most marvelous Matisse things on the wall. And they'd never come out," said Patricia. So they started to make sets for their friends. The thing snowballed.

In 1973, Colorforms branched out and made Shrinky Dinks, a hugely popular—and again, hugely simple—idea that became very popular. Shrinky Dinks were pieces of plastic made in the shape of whatever you want that are then placed in an oven. The heat of the oven shrunk the pieces of plastic so that they were around a third of their size but up to nine times thicker. Thus you could make pendants, ornaments, even sharp objects to throw at your brother…

✈ ✈ An E.T. Shrinky Dink
✈ Colorform set

ON FORM

Colorforms was one of the first toys to be promoted in TV commercials, and was the first to license characters with its 1957 Popeye cartoon kit. By 1991, it had sold over a billion sets. In 2004, a Beatles Colorforms set sold for $520.

GODZILLA

✈ ✈ ✈ A Mad Monster dinner-
dance gets under way

Back in the 1950s, Universal syndicated its classic monster movies to TV stations across the country and introduced "Horror Hosts" such as Vampira. Then came *Famous Monsters*, a magazine, and in 1961 Aurora Plastics made its first monster model kit—of Frankenstein's monster.

It was a huge success and a wave of monster merchandise followed. Monsters maintained their popularity into the 1970s and other companies, such as MPC, AHI, Lincoln and Fundimensions, made monster figures. Other monsters appeared, like the sci-fi-influenced Gigantic Insect Scenes. Aurora re-issued their early 1960s monster models in 1972, and introduced a new line of "Monsters From The Movies" models in 1975, with Godzilla being a major seller. Like many toy lines, though, they were effectively killed off by *Star Wars* in 1977.

REAL LIFE HEROES

EVEL KNIEVEL

**Ideal
1972–1982**

STUNT WORLD

The basic Evel and bike set cost $9.94. There was a dragster Funny Car ($9.94), a Stunt Cycle ($9.94), and Super Cycle with jet turbine engines that emitted real sparks ($12.94). There was even an Evel Knievel Stunt World Set (yours for $12.95) where kids could re-enact EK's amazing motorcycle leap across Idaho's snake river for which the real-life EK was paid a bionic $6 million.

There probably isn't a boy in the world, never mind America, who hasn't at some time set up a ramp, placed a few objects in front of it and tried to get a car or something to go up the ramp and jump over the objects. Why did we do this? What inspired this often mostly futile activity?

Evel chills by his
mobile home

Evel revs up
for a ramp jump
over rattlesnakes

A daredevil maniac with a name any metal band would kill for: Evel Knievel.

EK began his daredevil career in 1965 when he formed a troupe called Evel Knievel's Motorcycle Daredevils. His first stunts included jumping over live rattlesnakes (probably harder than it sounds) and being towed at 200 miles per hour behind dragsters. In 1972, Ideal released a 6" figure and more accessories than even the the most daring devil could jump over. The basic figure came with a helmet, white jumpsuit, shoes, and, curiously, a cane. His bottom was marked "1972 Ideal Hong Kong." His body was bendy with plastic hands and a vinyl head. There are a couple of jumpsuit variations. One was all blue and the other was made of a denim material.

In the late 1970s and early 1980s the Evel Knievel toys made over $300 million for the Ideal Toy Company and EK was credited with revitalizing an ailing industry.

Like the real thing, the Ideal Evel Knievel got knocked about a fair bit—it's an occupational hazard—and is now hard to find in mint condition. The wires in his limbs are often broken, the bottom of his helmet is usually cracked, and his cane is almost always missing. Figures in good condition can bring up to $100. In 1998, Playing Mantis reissued replicas of the original figure including the chopper bike.

THE BEATLES

Remco
1964–1969

There never was a
pop phenomenon like
The Beatles. Elvis
had been huge and
other pop stars
were influential,
but nothing
touched The
Beatles.

In 1964 Beatlemania really took off.
Milton Bradley made a Beatles board game called
Flip Your Wig, which looked a bit like a Monopoly with Moptop
pieces. Originally the game sold for $2.98, now a mint condition
set will go for nearer $400. Naturally, there were also Beatle
wigs—TV host Ed Sullivan jauntily wore one when introducing the
band on their second visit to his studio. Remco made a series of
Beatle dolls which were 5" tall, with a rubber or plastic body,
rubber heads and lifelike hair. Each had a black and gold plastic
instrument that bore their signatures (which was useful, because
they all looked the same). There was also a very rare custom
marked 5" Beatle Doll Set cardboard box.

Again in 1964—and this must have thrilled parents—came the
Beatles Bugle megaphone, made by the Yell-A-Phone Company of
Memphis. Originally there was a neck chain in a sealed envelope
inside the horn. Any surviving bugles with neck chains are now
worth a lot of dollars.

WE ALL LIVE IN...

Possibly the most recognizable
Beatle-related object is The Yellow
Submarine. Corgi's version (model
number 05403) came out in 1968
and the first edition—which is 50
times rarer than subsequent
editions—had a very short run.
The yellow and white hatches match
the color of the hull. A red strip
outlines the top half of the sub,
which is missing from later editions.
The original die-cast "Yellow
Submarine Plus Beatles Figures"
was re-issued in 1999 by Corgi
Classics, UK, as a limited edition
of 5,250.

Conceived by producers Bob Rafelson and Bert Schneider as a TV equivalent to Beatles films like *A Hard Day's Night*, *The Monkees* ran from September 12, 1966, to September 9, 1968.

On record, *The Monkees* were a commercial rather than a critical hit. Between 1966 and 1968, they had 11 Top 40 songs and sold over six million albums. On TV it was the other way round. The first show ranked only 70th on the influential Neilsens ratings chart, and yet *Monkees* TV tie-in merchandise was only surpassed by *Batman* and *The Man From U.N.C.L.E.* Games based on the series included The Monkees Game (Transogram, 1967) and The Monkees card game (Ed-U-Cards, 1967). Then there were Monkees Shades and a Monkees charm bracelet.

But it was only fitting that the Monkees' car proved to be the most enduring and the best of all the merchandise. NBC were given two 1966

Pontiac GTO convertibles by General Motors who said that they could do what they wanted with the cars as long as either of the words "Pontiac" or "GTO" was on the finished beast. Custom car designer Dean Jeffries created The Monkeemobile.

Corgi sold a 6" model (Corgi No:277) complete with four figures which, in mint condition, would now cost over $400. Airfix also made a model. And when CBS re-ran the series in the early 1970s, Monkeemobiles hit the stores once more.

The Monkeemobile—   ✈ ✈ ✈
still available to buy

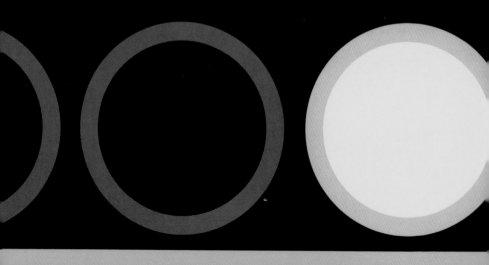

MATCHBOX CARS

Lesney Products & Co
1953–1992

It doesn't matter whether you've had one car or 41. It doesn't matter if you drive a sedate family sedan or a souped-up coupé with extra exhausts and spinning hub-caps. It doesn't matter because the odds are that the first car you owned was a Matchbox.

The company that would go on to make Matchbox cars was founded in 1947 by Rodney Smith and Leslie Smith (they weren't related; it's just everyone in England is called Smith) who formed a company called Lesney (their first names combined). They bought a second-hand die-cast machine and started to make electrical components.

A Matchbox Wells Fargo armoured truck

A Matchbox ambulance with Superfast wheels

BY ROYAL APPOINTMENT

Lesney's first toy was a tin-plate creature called Jumbo The Elephant which, though it sold well, wasn't going to really fly for them. They made anything they could sell and specialized in Royal souvenirs. In 1952, when Princess Elizabeth was crowned Queen Elizabeth II, they made a commemorative Royal coach. It sold by the bucket load. Lesney looked at this runaway success and realized that this was where the future lay. Not in Royal souvenirs, but in vehicles.

The first Matchbox cars were made in 1953—four models, the Muir Hill Site Dumper, the Road Roller, the Massey Harris Tractor, and the Cement Mixer—and were showed at the 1954 Harrogate Toy Fair. There was no packaging, so their new partner, Jack O'Dell, suggested they use a box "about the same size and shape as a matchbox."

Wanting to concentrate on production, Lesney sold 50% of the business to the Moko Company, who designed the packaging, boxes and logos. The toys took off. In 1956 they made an MG Midget car and opened up the American market.

Lesney owned the die-cast car market until 1969 when Mattel launched

Hot Wheels (see page 64). Flashier and hipper, they ate into Matchbox's market share. To counter this, Lesney designed their Superfast models which, like Hot Wheels, had whizzy wheels and could go super fast.

The 1970s proved to be a time of change for Lesney. In 1973, they released many new products including "Rolomatics," which had parts that moved as the wheels revolved, but production was hit by strikes, a fire, and a flood. The 1980s saw a series of takeovers and mergers that resulted in the company being owned by Universal Toys and production moved to the Far East, but it didn't work out and in 1992 Lesney was declared bankrupt and the company was sold to Tyco. Late in 1992 Tyco formed Matchbox Collectibles to create a nostalgic range of cars. In 1997 Mattel purchased Tyco for $755 million.

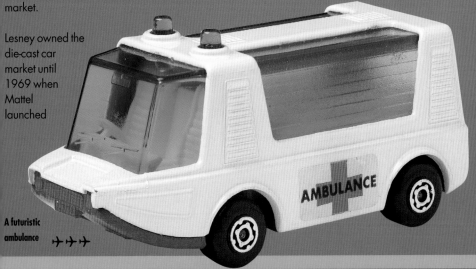

A futuristic ambulance ✈ ✈ ✈

HOT WHEELS

Mattel
1968–Present Day

In 1968 Mattel, one of the biggest toy companies in the world, revolutionized the die-cast car market when they launched Hot Wheels. Designed by Mattel founder Elliot Handler, they were stylish, detailed and modern: $\frac{1}{64}$-scale cars that moved at speeds far beyond their competition. In the mid-60s Californian hot rods were all the rage, and Hot Wheels mirrored that style: hot mag wheels, red-stripes on their tyres and "dazzling Spectraflame paint jobs." Their name comes from Handler who, legend has it, took one look at his new, ultra-fast car and said, "Wow, those are hot wheels."

The cars came with a plastic track and moved so fast that they could drive sideways and upside down if the track

ZOWEES

You couldn't get Zowees in shops—only as promotions at Shell Oil stations when you bought gas. You could get them free with a fill up or you could buy them for 49 cents. There were eight different Zowees, each in a plastic bag with a small paper ad stating that they were available from participating Shell dealers. The ad showed all eight Zowees. Later, five more models were added that sold in stores only.

✈ Hot Wheels were
✈ always fast looking
✈

HOT WHEELS

The rarest Hot Wheels car is a VW Beach Bomb, made in 1969. It had two surfboards mounted through the back window. Today it's worth up to $8,000.

was looped. The detailing on them was fantastic: side pipes, power bulges, exhaust pipes, vinyl tops, contrasting interiors. They sold faster than anyone dared hope. Sales were helped by a Hot Wheels TV show—until it was banned in 1969 by the Federal Communications Commission. They thought that it was all about selling Hot Wheels, apparently.

In 1998 Hot Wheels celebrated its 30th birthday with the sale of its two billionth car.

SIZZLERS—THE WORLD'S FASTEST ELECTRIC CARS!

Sizzlers were Hot Wheels with a rechargeable battery that could run and run around an oval track on a single charge. To

help their endurance, they were made of lightweight plastic instead of metal. Which means that unlike normal Hot Wheels cars, they're now incredibly difficult to find. There were three different ways to charge your Sizzler: The first was the Goose Pump. It contained two batteries in a red container with a small jack which you would plug into the side of the car. Then there was the Juice Machine, which looked like a gigantic gas pump. The third (and most expensive) was the deluxe Power Pit. This looked like a miniature gas station where your cars could pull off and recharge.

A sand buggy vs a monster truck

SLOT CARS

Various
1956–1977

The boom years following World War II saw the first big growth of slot cars. The idea had come from England where it had been a hit among model train hobbyists—the model car track system used a rail to control the vehicles, which were called, unsurprisingly, Rail Cars.

Slot-car racing was a relatively genteel pastime—rather like model trains—until it crossed the Atlantic, initially brought back by returning GI Joes. Americans organized the activity, making it large scale and commercial. Tom Cook of Kalamazoo, Michigan designed the first multi-lane ¹⁄₄₀-scale commercial raceway with his friends Harry Hedges and Bill Wilson. From there, it was a hop and a skip to competition and speed.

MOTORIFIC

Ideal's Motorific cars were powered by two AA batteries, had no contacts in the track and you couldn't control the car's speed. Great for crashing, not so great for actual driving. Made between 1965 and 1970, there were three different types: Motorific— designed as 'test tracks', with a variety of tests performed on the car; Racerific— which came with a timer so you could compete; Highway Sets— which had a larger track for trucks. They were called Torture Tracks.

✈ **The slot car pioneers**
✈ **were Brits—Scalextric**
✈

AMAZAMATIC

Not a slot car, but... Hasbro's Amaze-A-Matics were something else. A computer car, Amaze-A-Matics were advertised as "The Fantastic Car with a Brain!" Made from 1969, it was an 8" car that had a slot in the back. Feed your "computer card" into the slot and the car ran over it's newly programmed course. The courses included Le Mans, Sebring and Daytona, but the real joy was writing your own course on the (provided) blank cards. Do it right and you could whizz your Amaze-A-Matic round the house and have it return to you. Terrify the dog. Freak out the cat.

The early 1960s slot cars were simple affairs. The motor was generally taken from a rail train, and the slot guide was a pin with brushes on either side. Bodies were either plastic or nylon-covered balsa wood. But the joy of this toy was in customizing and making their car your car. In 1963 *Car Model* magazine showed that sales had hit the 100 million mark and that there were 20,000 commercial tracks. Slot-car racing was so popular that live television events were organized, hosted by top names like Steve Allen and Johnny Carson. Ed Sullivan hosted a race with the top drivers of the day, including Stirling Moss, Graham Hill, and Jackie Stewart. It was big.

Elvis had a slot-car room at Graceland with a 155ft track.

Like everything though, slot-car racing had its day and by the early 1970s most of the commercial tracks had been closed. By the end of the decade those tracks had probably been replaced by alien boxes bleeping, as the young boys who once flung their cars around raceways were in a different place, killing Space Invaders.

Pit stops were over in half a day

DINKY CARS

Hornby
1933–1980

CARS ON FILM

Like all toy manufacturers, Dinky realized that the future lay in producing cars of popular iconic film and TV characters. Following Corgi, they made a James Bond Aston Martin DB5, but unlike Corgi they had real wire spokes, opening doors and bonnet, tipping seats, dashboard, and gears. Curiously, they drew the line at an ejector seat.

In 1933, Frank Hornby's company (see Meccano, page 101) developed the Dinky car. "Dinky" being Scottish slang at the time for "cool."

Trucks, ambulances, fire engines, and the cars of the day rolled off the production lines. In 1947, Dinky Supertoys—large vehicles with their own die-cast wheel hubs and treaded rubber tires—were issued. In 1963, the British branch of Dinky Toys was bought by Tri-ang. Production was expanded. A factory in Hong Kong made cars especially for the US market. During the early 1960s, both Dinky and Corgi started to make their cars bigger—they were now $\frac{1}{35}$ scale instead of $\frac{1}{43}$. In 1967 Dinky made Superwheels, a response to Mattel's Hot Wheels. The first Dinky to be fitted with the new wheels was the Pontiac Parisienne. Next, they made the Dragster, which had a starter unit fitted with a spring. Mini-Dinky Toys appeared in 1968, each with its own plastic garage. Two racing cars in the series were made by Best Box of the Netherlands.

Dinky
TOYS ®

No9
3p

Tough
die-cast
metal
models

Dinky workmen
never stopped ✈ ✈ ✈

TC4

CONVEYANCER

CORGI

Mettoy Ltd
1956–Present day

The aerial rescue truck in action

Metttoy (metal toy) had been set up in 1936 in England to make metal toys. But it wasn't until 1954 that their first drawings for die-cast cars appeared. Realizing that copying the existing Dinky cars wouldn't be good enough, they decided to make cars with windows—and that became the company slogan "The First With Windows."

Mettoy branded the new range Corgi. On July 9 1956, the first Corgi car appeared. Sales for the first year reached 2.75million. Soon cars had not only windows, but seats, steering wheels and spring suspension.

The top model, with sales exceeding five million, is Bruce Wayne's 1966 Batmobile. Some of the most sought-after Corgis include the 1965 Monte Carlo Rally Mini Cooper S ($300–$400), 1966 The Man from U.N.C.L.E's Thrushbuster Oldsmobile ($250–$300), 1959-61 Ford Thunderbird Hardtop, pale green body ($175–$200).

007

Corgi has long had an association with British secret service agent James Bond. Still the company's best-known model is 007's gold-painted Aston Martin DB5. Produced in 1965, it sold more than 3.9 million in the next three years. Corgi has also made die-cast vehicles for *You Only Live Twice* (Toyota GT), *On Her Majesty's Secret Service* (bobsled), *Diamonds Are Forever* (moonbuggy), *The Spy Who Loved Me* (Lotus), *Moonraker* (shuttle), and *Octopussy* (BeeDee plane and trailer).

Always keep the original box

JOHNNY LIGHTNING

Topper Corporation
1969–1971

The Topper Corporation unveiled its Johnny Lightning brand in 1969, the year after Mattel brought out their Hot Wheels range (see page 64). They were metal cars which could be rolled by gravity or propelled around a track by a catapult device called an actuator. Because the actuator is hand operated, Topper claimed that Johnny Lightning races were won by skill. They also claimed that Johnny Lightning was faster than any Hot Wheels car—their secret being in the wheel construction: JL wheels were made of celcon and hung on straight axles.

Both companies advertised heavily—on TV, cereal boxes, badges, patches, coloring books. It was estimated that in 1969 Mattel spent more on advertising than some oil companies, while Topper puts almost a quarter of its gross income back into advertising. In May 1969 Topper sponsored the Johnny Lightning 500 car that Al Unser drove to victory at Indianapolis. Unser turned into Topper's chief marketing tool. But they still didn't win. The Topper Corp was liquidated in 1971.

PLAYING MANTIS

In 1993 Tom Lowe, the founder of the Playing Mantis Company, bought the rights to Johnny Lightning cars. Playing Mantis re-created eight of the original models and had them mass produced in China. These were launched in January 1994 as The Challengers. Next year The Challengers 1995 came out, and included the Custom Thunderbird.

A Playing Mantis Johnny Lightning model

TOOTSIETOYS

The Dowst Manufacturing Company Of Chicago
1922—Present Day

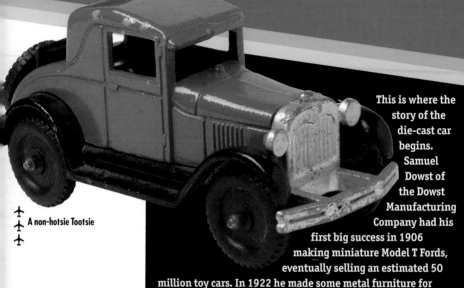

✈
✈
✈ **A non-hotsie Tootsie**
✈

This is where the story of the die-cast car begins. Samuel Dowst of the Dowst Manufacturing Company had his first big success in 1906 making miniature Model T Fords, eventually selling an estimated 50 million toy cars. In 1922 he made some metal furniture for dolls' houses. Looking for a name he chanced upon the granddaughter of his brother. Her name was Tootsie—and that furniture was the first Tootsietoy.

In 1934 the company (who had been bought out by Nathan Shure's Cosmo Manufacturing Company in 1926) changed the materials used in Tootsietoys from lead to mazac—a zinc-based alloy that was more durable and lighter. Despite the Depression, they survived by maintaining their penny toy ethos and diversifying into making planes and trains as well as cars and dolls' houses.

In 1961 NSCMC bought the toy line of the Strombeck-Becker company. It changed its name to the Strombecker Corporation but kept the Tootsietoys stamp on the bottom of its toys. Tootsies are still made today but the old lead toys are highly collectable.

DID YOU KNOW...

Samuel Dowst's first venture was a 'magazine' called the *National Laundry Journal*.

TONKA TOYS

Mound Metalcraft
1946–1991

Named after Lake Minnetonka in Minnesota, Tonka began life in 1946 as Mound Metalcraft, a company set up to manufacture garden instruments. When a client asked them to make steel toys, they came up with two models—the Steam Shovel and the Crane and Clam. These sold far better than any of Mound's gardening tools and soon the company's new line, now called Tonka Toys, was the dominant one.

In 1956, Tonka launched the Fire Engine, a bright cherry-red vehicle. It was hugely popular but incurred the wrath of parents when—legend has it—kids began starting real fires to test the toy. In 1964 the company's most successful toy made its first appearance: the yellow Mighty Dump Truck. It was so successful that in 1982—the same year Tonka introduced its first battery-powered toy, the Power Shift Mountain Master—the seven millionth truck rolled off the production line.

DID YOU KNOW...

The word "tonka" means great to the Dakota Sioux, the tribe native to Minnesota.

Tonka's corporate history is typical of companies in the games industry. It took over another company and went from strength to strength. (In 1988, Tonka swallowed up Kenner Parker Toys Inc. and that year sales exceeded $300 million.) Then in 1991 the by-now huge corporation was taken over by Hasbro and the Tonka corporation was duly swallowed.

⚓ The Mighty
⚓ Dump Truck
⚓

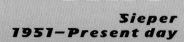

MAJORETTE (1961–1992)

French toy car manufacturer Majorette moved into the American market with the establishment of Majorette USA in Miami in 1982. Apart from the 600 Series, which has interesting-sounding models such as Road Eaters, Smelly Speeders and Sonic Flashers, most Majorette models are about 3" long and not dissimilar to Matchbox.

A Siku fire truck and (right) an original Siku ad

At first Siku, a German company, was known just for its margarine figures—so-called because the plastic toys were given away free with margarine. Siku began making fairly basic cars; a fire-engine in 1951, a racecar in 1952 and then a Porsche in 1955. The first American cars were a Buick Century in 1956, a Mercury Voyager in 1957, and a Chrysler New Yorker in 1960.

In the early 1960s, production was switched to die-cast metal and the number of plastic models was gradually reduced. Under 'attack' from Matchbox and Mattel's Hot Wheels, Siku adopted the philosophy "Kids want to play with what their parents drive" and launched the Super Series, producing popular German cars like the VW Beetle, Golf, Passat and Transporter, the Opel Kadett and Senator, the Porsche 911, and many Mercedes Benz models. They also made a range of trucks and emergency vehicles.

KNIGHT RIDER

Ertl
1983–1989

The K.I.T.T. (Knight Industries Two Thousand) car was the star of NBC's hit early 1980s show *Knight Rider*. An atypical black Pontiac Trans Am, its talking, computerized dashboard featured auto pursuit, emergency eject and X-ray surveillance systems. It could "fly" over obstacles, had a turbojet, and traveled at 300 MPH. Pontiac, which supplied the car used for K.I.T.T., found itself snowed under with orders for the black Firebird Trans Ams with T-tops, tan interiors, and red lights on the front bumper, just like the real thing.

Some customers had to settle for Ertl's lovingly crafted ⅛-scale die-cast model. Made in 1983, it was perfectly detailed. Press the license plate and it would say various things. There was also an action figure of Michael Knight.

KOJAK

Corgi
1975–1981
Mattel
1975–Present day

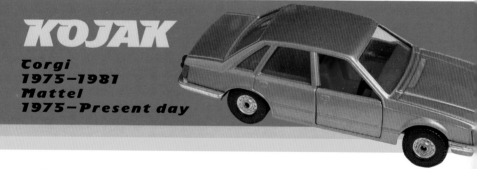

Kojak was a curious show. It created a star out of a far-from-obvious hero and it made a cult out of a hitherto unheralded car. But if a large bald man who went around sucking a lollipop could be a sex symbol, then (the thinking clearly went) a standard mid-size GM car could be up there

with Starsky's Ford Torino as a star of screen and street.

Corgi created a die-cast model of Kojak's 1975 Buick Regal (above), and Mattel's Hot Wheels version is still available today.

THE SAINT

258), but in 1966 they repainted their P1800 models in white, and added a Saint logo to the hood. In the 1980s a lead character in TV's *Thirtysomething* would drive the same car (minus the Saint logo, of course). The character was suitably saint-like.

When Roger Moore became the Saint in 1962, he was given one of the most beautiful sports cars ever built to drive: the Volvo P1800. Corgi already had a P1800 in their catalog (Corgi number

When the Saint returned to TV in the early 1980s Simon Templar was given a Jaguar XJS. Also white, it had the same logo as the 1960s car (pictured). It helped both sales of the new Jag coupé and the cool of the Saint, Ian Ogilvy.

THE DUKES OF HAZZARD

Hugely popular from 1979 to 1985, *The Dukes of Hazzard* was a curious show, but it made a star out of its iconic lead, an orange, 1969 Dodge Charger named The General Lee. It had fixed doors that everyone had to climb in and out of and a very strong suspension—which

was useful given how many times it leapt bridges and careered across fields.

Corgi Classics made a 1/36 scale—six inches long—die-cast model of the General Lee which came with hand-painted metal figures.

TRAINS

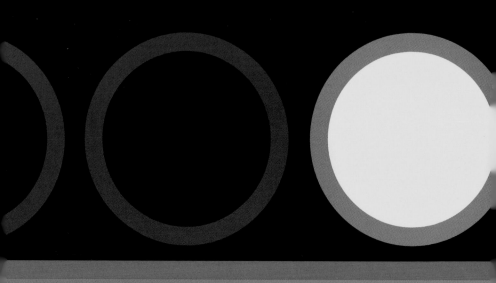

LIONEL TRAINS

The Lionel Manufacturing Company
1902–Present day

Young Joshua Lionel Cohen was seven when he built his first train. A steam engine attached to a wooden locomotive, it exploded in the family kitchen.

In 1902, The Lionel Manufacturing Company published its first trains catalog. Lionel Cowan (like a lot of Jewish immigrants, he changed his name to avoid anti-Semitic discrimination) left nothing to chance, and his first trains had both acid and lead plates to use in houses which had electricity, and dry-cell batteries for houses without. Lionel's two major breakthroughs came in 1934. Pullman built the M-10000 (The City of Salina) for Union Pacific. It was a revolutionary streamline train. Lionel copied it and it sold fantastically well. Also that year, Lionel made the Mickey and Minnie Mouse Handcar, a simple wind-up that ran on standard track. Typically, each one sold included a Lionel catalog.

In the 1950s, Lionel found things harder. Kids wanted cars and planes, not trains. Seeking a new market, in 1957 Lionel tried to appeal to girls and put out a pastel pink thing called The Girl's Train. Amazingly, it bombed. Now, of course, you can't get one for love or money. But Lionel wasn't finished and later that year produced the Super O track, which is still viewed by many collectors as the most realistic track system ever.

Lionel trains always ran on time, whatever the weather

RIVETTING

There's a fantastic story that reflects Lionel's legendary attention to detail. In 1937, the company put out an exact replica of New York Central's steam loco. Lionel claimed that its model had exactly the same number of rivets as the real thing: 1,600. One day a man—someone with a bit of time on his hands, presumably—counted the number of rivets of both model and train. Anyway, the train had 1,402 rivets. Lionel had 1,399. Immediately the company issued an apology and created a new job: rivet-counter.

You can touch this
+←+←+← third rail

MARX TRAINS

Where Lionel made trains that aspired to be like little versions of the real thing, Marx trains were toys. Louis Marx & Co. was founded in 1919 by Louis and David Marx and first produced trains in 1938. Marx made small O-gauge trains. They were a bit smaller than Lionel or American Flyer trains and sold for much less. But they weren't only cheap they were tough, too—probably tougher than their more expensive rivals. You could buy an entire Marx toy railway for the cost of one Lionel train set.

Marx probably sold more trains than Lionel, but they were never taken as seriously. Rather than get bogged down in detail and the number of rivets, Marx made stamped steel and tin lithographed versions of the popular trains of the day. One of the first was the Mercury, which was based on a New York Central streamliner.

liquidated the Marx assets. In the mid-1990s, though, a new Marx train appeared—a modern tin. These weren't reproductions because the details weren't the same. Neither do they appeal to collectors, since there is no shortage of old Marx trains.

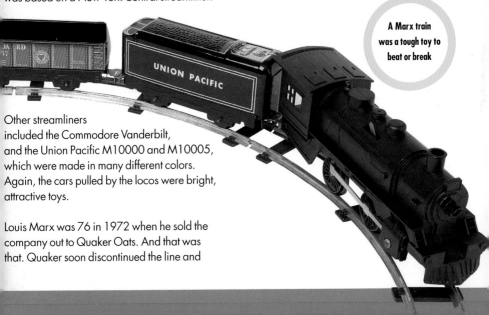

A Marx train was a tough toy to beat or break

Other streamliners included the Commodore Vanderbilt, and the Union Pacific M10000 and M10005, which were made in many different colors. Again, the cars pulled by the locos were bright, attractive toys.

Louis Marx was 76 in 1972 when he sold the company out to Quaker Oats. And that was that. Quaker soon discontinued the line and

AF TRAINS

American Flyer Company
1910–1966

AF Trains began life in 1910 when William Hafner sold half his clockwork toy company to Chicago hardware store owner William Coleman. They re-focused the company, called it American Flyer and turned it toward making clockwork trains. A good condition 1930s Flyer locomotive can now cost anything from $700 to $1,000.

In 1937, the company was bought by A.C.Gilbert, which had made its name making erector sets (see page 100). After the war the old methods and techniques of manufacturing were abandoned and the new wonder material—plastic—was used to produce accurately scaled trains that ran on a realistic two-rail system.

Whatever they did though, they never shared the popularity of Lionel trains. In 1961, a difficult time was made harder when A.C. Gilbert died. Jack Wrather, owner of the television series *The Lone Ranger* and *Lassie*, took over but four years later, after decades of trying unsuccessfully to save itself, Gilbert went out of business. In 1966, American Flyer was bought out by its long-time rival Lionel. They ended production of all flyer trains.

WHAT'S IN A LETTER?

First American Flyer and then A.C. Gilbert both fell foul of the gauge game. It started making 0- gauge trains when Lionel's HO trains were more popular. Then, after the War and

under new management, it decided to concentrate on the S gauge.

Though its attractive, well-made ³⁄₁₆" scale models had a good following, it could not compete with Lionel who, by now, had moved to 0 gauge and cornered the market at the expense of the incompatible S gauge trains. And that was the final nail in the freight.

TYCO TRAINS

Tyco
1952–1993

In 1926 John Tyler, James Thomas and Pauline Tyler got together and formed The Mantua Toy and Metal Products Company to make "Triple T Electrical Toys of Distinction." The company soon made its name as an innovator in the field of model railroading, producing miniature motors, steam locomotive and rolling stock kits, as well as some ready-to-run (R-T-R) locos and accessories. In 1952, they changed their name to TYCO (for Tyler Manufacturing Co.)

So the "blue-box era" began—so called because of the toys' light-blue packaging. TYCO offered kit versions and later R-T-R versions of various steam- and early diesel-era trains.

During the 1960s (the red-box era) TYCO added HO-scale slot-racing cars to their list. The HO-scale train line also saw growth and expansion. Consolidated Foods bought TYCO's model trains and slot cars around 1970 in what has come to be known, of course, as "The Consolidated Foods Era." Not only did this see

a change of color—brown this time—it also changed the company ethos. TYCO now offered a more "interesting" line including such items as a Popsicle and StarKist Tuna box cars.

> A Santa Fe line TYCO engine from the red box era

This attitude continued into the 1980s, with items like The A-Team and Rambo train sets. Meanwhile, TYCO diversified into different products, like Super Blocks (which were similar to Lego) telephones, and remote-control cars. The last appearance of a train in the TYCO catalog was in 1993. IHC—International Hobby Corporation—ended up owning this famous line of toy trains and carries on making trains today—minus the A-Team logo, of course.

MODEL TRAIN SETS

Revell, Mantua
1926–1960

The Californian-based company Revell, which made models and kits from the 1950s, is an important name in the history of model-making as it was there that the story of injection-moulded plastic (polystyrene) scale models began.

Back in the early 1950s, Lewis Glasser, the founder of Revell, decided to use injection-moulding equipment to make toys that could be put together with glue. The modeler could then paint the train using house paints or artists' oils. Curiously, Glasser had no interest in models himself and boasted that he'd never made one of his company's kits.

After the Tylers and Thomas had formed The Mantua Toy and Metal Products Company (see page 81) and sold their well-received miniature motors, steam loco and rolling stock kits, they introduced prefabricated switches and made Mantua's Ready-Laid Track, which was the first flexible track with brass rails. In 1936 they made their popular "Automatic Couplers"—which was another giant step forward in the modeling world.

A Revell steam engine model set

PEMCO

Distributed largely in Canada, Pemco—it stood for Precision Engineered Models Company— was an HO-scale model train line. Small and short-lived, it was conceived in the early 1980s as a line that would be aimed at the R-T-R toy train buyer, but made to a higher standard than the regular quality models.

IMPORTED TRAINS

In any form of collecting there's a value in rarity, a cachet in the exotic. And so it is with model trains. As good as American companies such as Lionel and American Flyer were, there was a big demand for models made by British companies like Hornby and Lone Star.

The Hornby company founder Frank Hornby had much in

Those were clockwork, and the first electric train appeared in 1925.

common with the American A.C. Gilbert. Both were restless businessmen and both had early success in the toy industry with construction kits—Gilbert with his Erector Sets, Hornby with Meccano. Both moved into toy trains.

Though some may have appeared before, the first catalogued date for a Hornby train is 1920.

In 1938, Hornby Dublo—a play on the Double-O gauge range—moved toy train production onto another level. The trains produced during the pre-WWII period are still highly sought after. Their now legendary model of the 1930s London to Scotland loco, the *Flying Scotsman*, is very collectible. However, things began to go wrong with the introduction of plastics in the late 1950s. Hornby was hit hard and in 1965 was taken over by Tri-ang.

A Tri-ang Hornby train from the 1960s

TRAIN ACCESSORIES

Atlas, Bachmann Brothers, Littletown
1947–Present day

It all began with a picket fence. Which is somehow fitting. In the post-war period, the explosion in plastics caused a revolution in the model train world. Not just in the actual trains—the rolling stock—but in all the accessories and related products. After all, as beautiful and detailed as the trains are, part of the fun is in creating an environment.

Through companies such as Atlas, Marx, K-Line, Plasticville (the clue's in the name) and Bachmann you could turn your living room floor into a town, complete with buildings, maybe a farm and some animals, a school, a church, even some people. You could create your own world. Plasticville was produced by Bachmann Brothers Inc., which had been founded in 1833 but didn't make plastic products until 1947. The first item was a picket fence.

A plastic engine could be painted more easily

A lovely plastic
station set ✈ ✈ ✈

The Atlas Model Railroad Company, Inc., was founded in 1924 by Stephan Schaffan Sr, a Czech immigrant who was a skilled tool-maker. In 1933, he was joined by Stephan Schaffan Jr, his son. Junior built model airplanes and, after a conversation in his local hobby shop, turned his hand to trains. In the 1930s, modelers had to assemble and build everything themselves. Junior—by now called Steve—saw an opening. He built the first "switch kit," developed a method of stapling rail to fibre track, and invented the first practical rail joiner and pre-assembled turnouts and flexible track.

Atlas radically changed the modeling world, and made flexible and reliable track. In time the company naturally moved to other areas and started to build actual trains. In 1985 Steve was inducted into the Model Railroad Industry Hall of Fame in Baltimore and in 1995 honored by the National Model Railroad Association Pioneers of Model Railroading.

Between 1952 and 1954 Louis Marx produced a line of plastic railroad buildings with and without figures and accessories under the name Marxville. Most of these buildings were relatively simple and used as a logical extension of the Marx line of model trains.

Atlas and Bachmann
trains ✈ ✈ ✈

PLANES
&
BOATS

AIRFIX

Airfix Industries 1939–1981

When Hungarian businessman Nicholas Kove founded his company in 1939 he called it Airfix so that it would always be the first mentioned in any trade catalogs.

The business was originally set up to make cheap rubber toys filled with air. After buying one of the first injection-moulding machines in England, Airfix moved into plastics and in 1948 were commissioned by Ferguson to make a promotional plastic toy tractor. Kove, realizing that this was not an economic idea, decided to sell it in kit form. The first Airfix kit proper was Sir Francis Drake's ship *The Golden Hind*. Carefully packaged, the kit was presented to the chainstore Woolworth's who liked it, but not at the proposed price. So Kove dropped the packaging and presented the kit in a clear plastic bag.

After Kove died in 1957, the company went public and formed Airfix Industries. In the early 1960s they moved into model railways and rolling stock kits with the Tank Wagon and Cement Wagon. In 1971 Airfix bought Meccano and Dinky. Later that year, it was awarded the Queen's Award to Industry for export achievements. In 1981 the company went bust.

A commercial airliner kit from Airfix

SPITFIRE

In 1953, Airfix produced its first aircraft, the Spitfire Mk 1. The remoulded kit is still in the Airfix range today.

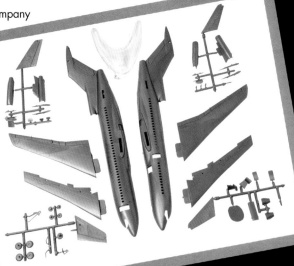

The advert for Kenner's Car-Plane proudly proclaimed that, "Child pilots plane from inside car window." It was one of those things that probably seemed a good idea at the time.

Retailing for $2.98, the Car-Plane was a curious kind of remote-control toy. It hung outside the car connected by what looked like a crane. This was actually a tube that connected the plane to a support and then to a hand-held control panel. Little Johnny held the control panel and when the car had gained enough speed and there was enough air resistance he could launch the plane!

BUBBLE-MATIC!

Kenner's first toy, made in 1947, was the Bubble-Matic Gun—which fired bubble-gum. Fire it against the wind and the pellet remains a lump of bubble gum; fire it with the wind and a huge bubble emerges... Kenner wasn't all quirk, though. In 1956 it introduced Play-Doh.

Where did the launched plane go, though? Actually, it went nowhere except where your car was going. The "remote control" would give wind velocity readings and you could point the plane up or down, left a bit and right, but it stayed stuck on the wire, outside your car window. Unless Pop drove too close to another vehicle, of course, and then it was gone...

HUBLEY PLANES

The Hubley Manufacturing Company 1940–1965

"They're different." It might not be the snappiest motto ever invented, but it seemed a good one to John E. Hubley. Back in 1894, he set up the Hubley Manufacturing Company to make toys that worked using the new-fangled electricity. And if they worked on electricity, they would indeed be different from all the other cast-iron and clockwork toys around.

Hubley soon made a name for itself producing toy trains, but that reputation was wrecked in 1909 when a fire demolished its factory. When the company acquired new premises Hubley concentrated on cast-iron toys—cars and guns and novelties. Cars were the company's biggest seller until, post-WWII, it moved into making the planes that the war had made glamorous. In the immediate post-war period, Hubley planes proved to be the standard. Small and simple and with their trademark folding wings, they were accessible and easy to use. Hubley was bought out by Gabriel Industries in 1965.

A Hubley replica
Hellcat "Indian"—
early 1990s

HUBLEY'S FLYING CIRCUS

In the 1940s and 1950s, Hubley made airplanes that looked like they'd been made in the cast-iron style, but were actually a light alloy. One of the best of this period is the Lockheed P-38, which had retractable gear and spinning props. The Flying Circus P-40s were a companion plane to the P-38. Made in the US, the hand-painted P-40s had both a three-blade and (rarer) a two-bladed prop. The wingspan was 8¼". Unlike the P-38, the gear does not retract. Both these planes were made continuously from 1940 through to the 1970s.

The post-WWII revolution in plastics had a major impact on toy makers, particularly those who specialized in transportation toys. Big companies such as Monogram, Aurora, Pyro, and Revell thrived on plastic technology. It was estimated that, in 1951, not only were Revell making more cars than Ford, General Motors, and Chrysler combined, they were also producing more planes than the entire air industry.

One of Revell's most popular models was the ⅟₄₈ B17-G Flying Fortress (855600)—itself one of the most famous aircraft from WWII. Its features included a detailed interior, gunner stations, cockpit, and landing gear. It was just over 19" long and had a wingspan of 26".

One of Revell's most successful kits

SHOOTING STAR

† Catch a fallin

The first model airplane clubs started around New York at the turn of the 20th century. Initially, model planes were made of bamboo, pine, and spruce, and it wasn't until 1911 that balsa wood was used. As the hobby grew, different model plane schools evolved. You could make your plane, fly your plane or simply admire your plane.

Younger kids could join in with toys such as the Rocket-Plane Launch Set, a light plastic plane that sat on a stand which was attached to an air pump. Jump on the air pump and… off goes your plane. Similarly, with its 19" wingspan the Cox "gas-powered" plane could take off if you swung it round hard enough. That "not to be used without adult supervision" label? Hey, who saw that?

Die-cast planes were—and remain—more for collectors than players. Companies such as Corgi and Dinky were very active in the field, and began producing die-cast aircraft prior to WWII. One of the most popular Dinky series were the "Skybusters." There were four planes—Corsair, RamRod, Wild Wind and Cessna Twin—with their own airport and two runways.

TOP GUN

One of the most important American war planes (a.k.a. Warbirds) was the Lockheed Shooting Star. It was the States' first operational jet fighter when it went into service on January 8, 1944 and, in full *Top Gun* style, came out on top in the world's first all-jet combat when it destroyed a Russian MiG-15 fighter in the Korean War. Dinky immortalized the Shooting Star (model number 773) in 1954 and in good condition it is very collectible. One of the rarest die-cast planes is the Dinky Vulcan bomber. Just 500 of these were made in Canada, and in good condition can go for up to $4,000.

Aeroclassics was started in 1999 by Andrew Klein to make classic aeros, that's to say retro model aircraft dating from the 1950s through to the modern day, but concentrating on the 1960s and 1970s.

Even though the company has been active for a relatively short period of time, their early models—the First Generation, such as the Eastern Airlines DC-6 and the Vickers VC-10—go for big money in the auction market. The Vickers is especially rare because not only was it produced in a limited run, it was also a troubled production and many were melted down due to a perceived lack of quality.

By 2002, demand for Aeroclassics model planes had increased to such a level that production moved to China where bigger runs and lower costs could be achieved. The Second Generation launched with the Quebecair BAC-111, and a range of DC-9-10s and BAC-111s.

Later that year, a new model was introduced: the injection-moulded printed model. The process of manufacturing allowed for much greater stability and detail. They weren't spin-cast and (for collectors the main give-away) didn't have a screw at the bottom. The first models produced using this method were the SE-210 Caravelle and the Boeing 707-400.

Not really a toy: an Aer Lingus 707

PROMOTIONAL AIRPLANES

Various
1930s–Present Day

Maybe of more interest to collectors than the kid in the street, one of the more popular uses for model planes was as a promotional tool.

Planes have been used for promotional purposes since the 1930s when Zeppelins were used, both as cast figures and as more regular toys, but they really took off (sorry) in the 1960s. As the 1950s drew to a close, the popularity of die-cast planes fell away as air travel became more affordable and therefore commonplace. The Jet Set had lost some of its newness and appeal by the 1960s while the idea of space travel was new and irresistible. Planes had become just another form of transport. Spaceships were the new, must-have toy for boys. So the new market for planes became the adult-oriented promotional one.

Typically, promotional planes were metal and made by companies such as Corgi, though in the 1970s Bachmann made a small-scale range in plastic. Today the tradition is continued through companies such as GeminiJets, Herpa, and JustPlaneModels. These take a particular pride in their delicate quality and specialize in wonderfully intricate models in a variety of materials, from resin, plastic and metal to kiln-dried mahogany.

Who wouldn't want this on their desk?

AIRPORT PROMO

It wasn't just planes. Marx, for one, made a model airport for Trans-American Airways in the early 1930s. Made of tin and measuring 12" by 6.75" by 4", it comprised the main airport building with sign on the windows for the ticket office, radio room, restaurant and so on. There were two hangars next to the building. The Trans-American Airways logo is written on the runway.

BALSA WOOD AIRPLANES

Nu Craft Toys
1926–Present Day

OCHROMA LAGOPUS

Otherwise known as Balsa wood, this is the third lightest wood in the world. It grows naturally in the humid rain forests of central and South America. The primary source of model-aircraft grade balsa is Ecuador. The word balsa is Spanish and means raft, in reference to its excellent flotation qualities. In Ecuador it is known as Boya, meaning buoy.

A balsa wood Spitfire

In 1926 America was aircraft mad and Paul K. Guillow, a WWI US Navy pilot, combined his hobby with his job and set up a company called Nu Craft Toys. He went to market with a small wooden plane that he'd designed.

In 1927 Charles A. Lindbergh flew from New York to Paris, the first successful solo flight across the Atlantic. Interest in aviation peaked. Guillow's model airplane kits took off. His first line consisted of 12 different WWI biplane fighters with 6″ wingspans. They sold for 10¢ each.

After a dip during WWII when balsa wood was in short supply, the business soared again. A new "stick and tissue" technique was developed and the familiar rubber band to wind up the propeller was introduced. Unlike many other toys, the basic design never changed. Small adjustments were made—size, color, shape—but the design was perfect. It was easy to use and inexpensive.

TOY BOATS

Remco, Tri-ang
1950–1965

At the turn of the century, when American companies like Lionel got heavily into making tin models, ships weren't really a part of the story. Shortly after World War I, though, Samuel Orkin, an engineer from Massachusetts who called himself The Toy Wizard, built working models of real US naval vessels—dreadnoughts, cruisers, destroyers, submarines. He built them big and on a small budget—and they sold well. Another company who made model boats during this period was the Walbert Manufacturing Company of Chicago. Their big toy was the "Sinking Battleship with Torpedo" in 1915. With this, you could "fire" the torpedo at the ship which, when hit, split and sank.

As with planes, the leaps in die-cast technology and materials didn't really help sales. One of the problems with die-cast boats was that if you played with them in their natural environment they sank. Die-cast boats were, and remain, things to lovingly collect and treasure rather than play with. In the 1940s though, the growth of the plastics industry made water-borne die-casts more achievable and companies such as Ideal and Dillon-Beck moved into making toys that could be played with at bath-time.

In the late 1950s and 1960s, manufacturers combined plastics and wood to make some beautiful working boats. The French company GeGe, Tri-ang in the UK, and Remco in the US were among those who made boats with wind-up motors that you could take out onto the local lake—or simply play with at home.

GOING UNDER

Sutcliffe, an old English company whose roots were in the sheet metal business, had a long tradition of making boats, to which they added a series of clockwork submarines in the 1950s. Three stand out: the grey and red Unda-Wunda which was made between 1948 and 1967; the Sea-Wolf submarine made between 1963 and 1981; and the Nautilus submarine which was a tie-in with the Disney film *Twenty Thousand Leagues Under the Sea*.

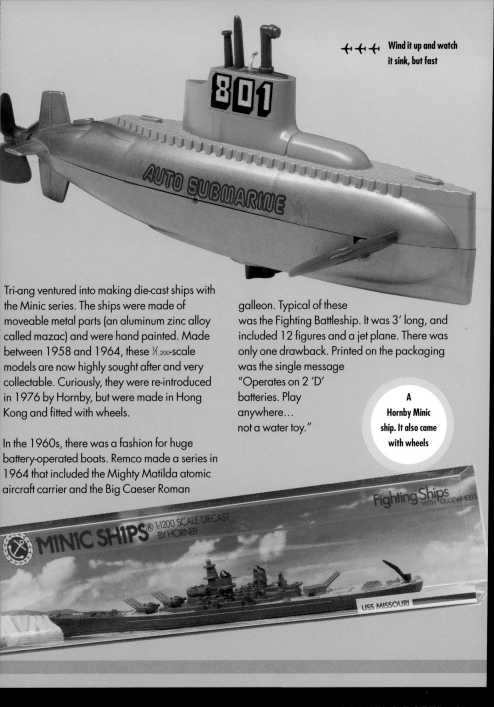

801

AUTO SUBMARINE

Wind it up and watch
it sink, but fast

Tri-ang ventured into making die-cast ships with the Minic series. The ships were made of moveable metal parts (an aluminum zinc alloy called mazac) and were hand painted. Made between 1958 and 1964, these $\frac{1}{1,200}$-scale models are now highly sought after and very collectable. Curiously, they were re-introduced in 1976 by Hornby, but were made in Hong Kong and fitted with wheels.

In the 1960s, there was a fashion for huge battery-operated boats. Remco made a series in 1964 that included the Mighty Matilda atomic aircraft carrier and the Big Caeser Roman galleon. Typical of these was the Fighting Battleship. It was 3′ long, and included 12 figures and a jet plane. There was only one drawback. Printed on the packaging was the single message "Operates on 2 'D' batteries. Play anywhere… not a water toy."

A
Hornby Minic
ship. It also came
with wheels

Fighting Ships WITH GUIDEWHEELS

MINIC SHIPS® 1:1200 SCALE DIECAST
BY HORNBY

USS MISSOURI

CONSTRUCTION
& MECHANICS

THE GILBERT ERECTOR SET

A.C. Gilbert
1913–1966
Hornby
1901–1981

To look back at his life, you'd think Alfred Carlton Gilbert was the kind of guy who'd disappear into a telephone booth at the drop of a hat, whip his clothes off and reveal a rather fetching blue and red lycra outfit.

✠ A vintage Gilbert
✠ Erector Set
✠

A.C. Gilbert made what are considered some of the best model trains ever (The American Flyer), a glass blowing kit, chemistry sets (including, curiously for the toy industry, one for girls in 1958), and an Atomic Energy Lab complete with real radioactive particles and a working Geiger counter (1950–52). By the time he died in 1962, Gilbert was credited with 150 patents for the inventions that went into his products. He considered his products were more than just "good, clean fun toys" he required that they not only entertain kids, but better their minds, too. He was the subject of a 2002 TV movie, snappily titled *The Man Who Saved Christmas*, starring Jason Alexander and Ed Asner. If you want to know more about the man, visit A.C. Gilbert's Discovery Village in Salem, Oregon.

HELLO BOYS!

The Erector Set was launched with the first national advertising campaign ever created for a toy. The sales line was "Hello Boys! Make Lots of Toys."

A.C. Gilbert was in fact a medical doctor—though he never practised. He broke the world record for pole vaulting at the 1908 Philadelphia Olympic trials, and tied for gold at the London Olympics the following year. He also revolutionized the sport by inventing the "box" the pole is put in by the vaulter. Plus, he was also an accomplished magician.

In 1910 Gilbert began making and selling magic kits under the name of The Mysto Manufacturing Company, and it was this that whetted his appetite for business. Legend has it that in 1911 Gilbert was on a train when he saw some workmen carrying the riveted steel beams of an electrical power line and, in one of those "Eureka!" moments, he decided to create a children's construction kit. It's also possible that he'd heard of a British company called Meccano which had started making a construction kit for children in 1901, but that's not such a good story.

Unlike Meccano, Gilbert's steel beams were not flat but bent at a 90 degree angle, so that four

of them side-to-side formed a sturdy, square, hollow support beam. He also thought it a good idea to make the toy move and so included an electric motor in each set sold. The Gilbert Erector Set was shown at the 1913 New York Toy Fair. Medicine's loss was every American boy's gain.

Five years after his death, the A.C. Gilbert toy company was bankrupt. The Gilbert and Erector names were bought first by Gabriel Toys, and then Ideal Toys.

Classic-era Meccano boxes

MECCANO

There were other erector sets, other manufacturers, but if it wasn't Gilbert, it was Meccano. Frank Hornby obtained the patent for it in 1901 and the first set went on sale in that year. It was first called Meccano in 1907.

While the American market pretty much belonged to A.C. Gilbert, Hornby went after the rest of world. Meccano was exported to Canada, Australia, New Zealand, India and made in other countries, such as France, Spain, and Argentina. For a few years there was a Meccano factory in New Jersey, but it didn't last long.

Plastic Meccano was introduced in 1965, largely to appeal to younger kids. Three years later, they introduced girls Meccano. There was also the Percy Train Set, a Meccano-based set for kids.

There were some specialty sets produced, such as the Aeroplane Constructor, Motor Car Constructor, Electrical, Army, Combat and Highway Vehicle sets. In 1979 the Space 2501 Set was introduced, without a motor.

The Meccanoids Set, introduced later that year, included the Crane motor to power a number of imaginative creatures from outer space. It was all to no avail, however, and in 1981 Meccano Ltd. went bust.

STILL BUILDING

Meccano, France, bought the rights to the Erector trademark in America and started selling Meccano sets marked Erector Meccano in 1979. Exacto Ltd, of Buenos Aires, Argentina, still produces the original Meccano.

Is it a Da Vinci? No, a Junior Meccano helicopter

VIEW-MASTER

When organ-maker William Gruber first conceived of the idea, his invention was to be a souvenir, something for tourists. He had the idea of taking the stereoscope and updating it with the new Kodachrome color film that had just hit the market. He wanted to mass-produce 3-D images and create a small viewing device. One day, while visiting local attraction Oregon Caves, he met Harold Graves, the president of Sawyer's Inc., a company that specialized in picture-postcards. Graves was taken by the idea but explained that he couldn't pay Gruber for it, only offer a share in future profits. William said yes.

View-Master and disks

The first reels produced by the new View-Master company showed beautiful scenery and lovely views: national parks, the Grand Canyon, and so on. Things took off during WWII though, when View-Master was taken on by the army who used it as a visual aid, for plane and ship identification. It was good for business—the military ordered millions of reels—and it was good for future business—so many people had seen the reels that, when the War ended, the company didn't need to market the device. In 1951 View-Master bought out their one major competitor, Tru-Vue, because they held the license to use Disney characters. From then on View-Master could produce reels for both adults and children.

STRAIGHT TO VIEW

Back in the 1960s, TV shows that bombed went straight to View-Master. *The Smith Family* (starring Henry Fonda), *Korg 70,000 B.C., Apple's Way, Julia* and *Isis* are a few of the forgotten shows that ended up on a reel.

For any building accidents, you'll need a hospital

In 1932 Danish carpenter Ole Kirk Christiansen was forced to diversify when hard times hit his business. He started to make stepladders, ironing boards and wooden toys. The ladders did well, the ironing boards less so. But what really sold were the wooden toys. He made small animals, little trucks, and small bricks. It occurred to Christiansen that his future lay in toys.

By 1934 his company was established. Unfortunately, tragedy struck in 1942 when Christiansen's factory burnt to the ground. But he rebuilt and re-organized, putting in first an assembly line and later a plastic injection-moulding machine.

In 1949 the company introduced what we now know and love as Lego. The Automatic Building Brick came in a set of stackable interlocking red and white bricks which were studded on top and hollow underneath. Things moved up a gear when Godtfred Kirk Christiansen (son of Ole Kirk) became Junior Vice President. He knew the business and had been working at the company since the age of 12. He changed the name of the product to "Lego

ASHES TO PLASTIC

After wood was abandoned (there was another fire in 1960) a material called cellulose acetate was used to make Lego bricks. This was, in turn, replaced in 1963 by acrylonitrile butadiene styrene, which made Lego brighter and stronger while adding to the versatility and strength of the brick. The manufacturing process of Lego is now so precise that on average, only 26 out of every 1,000,000 bricks made are rejected.

Mursten" (Lego Bricks) and introduced the "LEGO System of Play" comprising 28 sets and eight vehicles with extra parts. It allowed a child to expand and create their own world without a strict set of guidelines. By the 1950s Lego was sold all over Europe and, in 1961, was finally released in America. The following year Lego took delivery of its first plane and had to build a private airstrip to deal with the increased travel and shipping.

The next major development for Lego came in 1967 (in 1969, overseas) when the company released the Duplo brand. This was a larger brick, designed specially for children under five. It was a huge success. In 1995 Duplo Baby was created for the six-month to two-year-old market.

It starts so simply ...

DID YOU KNOW...

The name Lego comes from the two Danish words "leg" and "godt," which translate as "play well." It was only later that the company realized that the Latin translation is, "I put together." Fitting, really.

It has been calculated that six 8-stud bricks of the same color can be re-arranged in 102,981,500 different ways.

For the really heavy lego jobs, build a forklift

COMPUTING

ATARI CX40 JOYSTICK

Atari
1972–Present day

Way back in 1972, computers were still so big that they filled warehouses. The idea of making a game of one seemed impossible...

But Nolan Bushnell and Ted Dabney set up a company called Atari and within five years they'd created an entire industry. Such was its growth that in 1976 along came Warner Comunications and, PacMan-style, gobbled up Atari for $28milllion.

Atari's first big seller was the 2600 console (originally called the VCS), a wooden box that went on to sell over 30 million units. Some of the 2600's controllers—joysticks—were game-specific, but the one that really took off was the CX40 (pictured).

You can now buy the joystick as the Atari 10-in-1, which comes pre-loaded with ten vintage games—Asteroids, Adventure, Missile Command, Centipede, Gravitar, Yar's Revenge, Breakout, Pong, Circus Atari, and Real Sports Volleyball. It plugs directly into a TV and includes everything you need to play. All for under $25.

PACMAN

There's a school of thought that says that the Atari 2600 was the main contributor to the great video game market crash of 1983-4. In 1982 Atari released Pac Man. The company expected it to sell by the bucket and were counting on about 20 million sales. It didn't take off to that extent though, and sold only 7 million. To make up the shortfall in expected revenue, Atari paid out for a license to create a game around the film *E.T.* Again, it didn't take off and shops were left with shelves of the thing. Burnt twice, the video game market was in tatters.

To its supporters, the Apple II was the Model T Ford of the computer world. In 1975 Apple had grown out of the Homebrew Computer club in Palo Alto, California. Steve Wozniak and Steve Jobs had designed the arcade game Breakout for Atari and decided to push ahead with their own designs. They began working on the original Apple computer (which came in a wooden box) and on April 1st, 1976 they formed the Apple Computer Company.

In May 1976 the Apple I went on sale for $666.66, assembled

with 4K of RAM. A low-cost MOS Technology 6502 microprocessor was used instead of the more popular but, at $179 more expensive, Intel 8080 processor.

The Apple II was launched at the First West Coast Computer Fair in April of 1977. It was an instant hit. The design appealed to people who knew nothing about computers. The insides, with easy access and eight expansion slots, appealed to people who did. Then there was the color logo. By 1993, when Apple had decided the II had gone mouldy, more than 5½ million customers had taken a bite.

SIMON

Milton-Bradley
1978–1985

Simon was a battery-operated game that took advantage of the burgeoning interest in computers. It was not complicated, though. It was, as the nursery rhyme had it, simple. The idea was that when you started Simon up, one of the four coloured

panels would light up and sound a tone. You then pressed the panel that lit up. Then another panel would light up. You press it. Then another. Then another. Then another. Until you missed. Then Simon would make a harsh buzzing noise. In 1979, MB released Super Simon for two people and then in 1980, Pocket Simon, which, of course, is smaller.

COMMODORE PET

**Commodore
1977–1985**

First shown at the 1976 Comdex electronics fair and introduced in 1977, the Commodore Pet was one of the first non-kit computers ready to use out of the box—all you had to do was plug in and play, as the later jargon would have it.

Commodore founder Jack Tramiel—an uncompromising businessman whose motto was "Business is war"—wasn't sure of the PET's potential to turn a profit though, and so ran a series of newspaper ads offering it for the lowest price he could: $599. Shortly after the ads appeared, Commodore received $3million worth of orders. That reassured Jack.

Designed by Chuck Peddle, who also designed the 6502 microprocessor which was used in many computers of the period including Apple, Atari and Commodore, the PET (Personal Electronic Transactor) came with a 9" integrated blue and white monitor, a main board with a powerful new 1Mhz MOS 6502 processor, room for an additional RAM or Processor board, 4K of memory, power supply, a real storage device (cassette tape), several expansion ports including an RS232 (serial) port, and an operating system that was burned onto ROM and loaded on boot. Uniquely, its cover could be lifted off— rather like a car bonnet—for servicing the computer.

BASIC MATH

The BASIC computer language that the PET used was written by an unknown little company called Microsoft. Clever Jack Tramiel bought BASIC outright on license. Which means that they only had to pay for versions written for the early models. Which meant that they could write as many future versions as they wanted without being subject to a license fee. And given that we're talking about literally millions of Commodore computers using a version of Microsoft BASIC, that's a lot of money that Bill Gates didn't get. (Don't worry: he made up for it later.)

**The PET:
unlike any pet you
ever owned
before**

SPECTRUM ZX

Meanwhile in Europe, Clive Sinclair's Spectrum company was setting the standard and as the 1980s began the most popular computer was his Spectrum. There were two models: one with 16 kb RAM and one with 48 kb RAM. Launched in 1982, it quickly spread across the Atlantic and 17 months after its release, sales had reached the one million mark. As a computer it was really quite limited, but it excelled at graphics and games. This, added to its price—under $200—and its stark black design, made it popular with the younger market.

The Spectrum was nothing if not quirky, though. One of its most interesting characteristics was the keyboard: it had rubber keys loaded with colorful inscriptions relating to their five different functions. The screen was divided in two parts: 22 lines were used to display the program listing and 2 lines at the bottom for the statements.

TANDY TRS-80

Nicknamed Trash-80 by the opposition, the TRS-80 was announced in New York on August 3, 1977, and deliveries started two weeks later. Two versions were sold: the keyboard/computer for $399 or the full version with display and cassette storage unit for $599. The system featured a 4 KB Level 1 Basic and 4 KB of RAM.

Retail chain Radio Shack—the owners of Tandy—were cautious (it was the most expensive thing they'd sold) and planned to sell about 600 to 1,000 in the first year. In the first month they received more than 10,000 orders.

The Model 1 became the ancestor of a dynasty of TRS computers, but was discontinued in 1981 because it never met the American FCC's Radio Frequency Interference rules.

PONG

Atari
1972–1977

In the beginning there was Pong. The joy of the game was its simplicity. There were no frightening graphics, no fancy lights, nothing. It was just a very basic, very slow game of table tennis on the telly. An instruction on the machine reading "Avoid missing ball for high score" was about as complicated as things got.

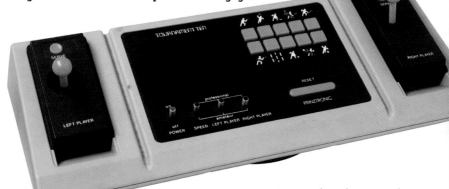

A game of skill and wits. Kinda like table tennis

Pong was first tested at a bar called Andy Capp's Cavern in Sunnyvale, California, and it was there that the world changed. Legend has it that the next day people were waiting outside the Cavern at 10AM, eager to play the new game.

The next major development in the story was in 1975 when Atari released the home version of Pong they'd been working on since 1973. Sold under license to Sears for their Tele-Games label ("Fast-paced games you play on your own TV,") it was a huge hit. Every Christmas has its "must-have" toy and in 1975 that toy was Pong. For the small matter of $98.85 you could be the coolest kid on the block.

Video game pioneer and founder of Atari, Nolan Bushnell, invented his first video game in 1970. Called Computer Space it was itself a version of another game, Space War, which had been written in the late 1960s. Computer Space had buttons called things like Rocket Thrust Control and Rocket Steering Control. This was all far too complicated, Bushnell thought. As he said, "To be successful, I had to come up with something so simple that any drunk in any bar could play."

Although Pong was very gentle, the first wave of home computer games were anything but. Each involved blowing something up or "killing" the enemy. Which is why boys loved them.

In 1978, Japanese company Taito produced a game called Space Invaders which took Japan by storm. Two years later, Atari secured the license and almost immediately sales of the Atari 2600 (see page 108) quadrupled. Space Invaders was to prove the most successful video arcade game for several years running and almost single-handedly created the US home video game market. Its success forced Pong into cupboards across the nation until, many years later, in a fit of fevered but short-lived nostalgia, owners would get the game out and attempt to relive their youth.

How early computer games looked ✈✈✈✈

DESIGN
CLASSIC

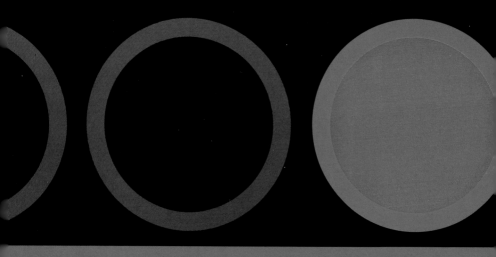

SLINKY

James Industries
1945–Present day

In 1945, Richard James, a naval engineer from Pennsylvania, was conducting an experiment in monitoring horse-power on battleships. When he accidentally dropped a tension spring on the floor he noticed how it seemed to walk as gravity took it on its path.

Just before Christmas 1945, a nervous James persuaded Gimbel's Department Store in Philadelphia to demonstrate his 80 feet of blue-black Swedish steel wire—a toy his wife Betty had named The Slinky. They sold 400 Slinkys in just 90 minutes. By 1956 James Industries was an internationally successful business that would sell over a quarter of a billion Slinkys across the globe.

ETCH-A-SKETCH

Ohio Art Company
1960–Present day

The world's first laptop, Etch-a-sketch is the red plastic draw-on, shake-off pad that has been keeping kids busy in the back of the car since the 1960s. It was invented in the late 1950s by a French garage mechanic, Paul Chasse, who named it L'Ecran Magique, The Magic Screen.

It was exhibited at the 1959 International Toy Exhibition in Nuremburg, Germany where scouts from The Ohio Art Company bought the rights for $25,000. After a re-design and change of name, Etch-a-sketch was introduced on July 12, 1960 retailing at $3.99.

MOUSETRAP

Milton Bradley
1963—Present day

You start by turning the crank that rotates the gears, that push the lever, that pushes a stop sign against a shoe that kicks the bucket holding a metal ball, that sends the ball down the stairs and into the gutter and onto a large hand, which nudges a rod that releases a second ball that falls through the bathtub and onto the diving springboard that catapults the diver through the air and into the washtub that causes the cage to fall and capture a mouse. Hmmm.

I would have loved to be at the ideas meeting when that was first suggested.

Introduced in 1963, Mousetrap was an immediate success. Parents loved "The crazy game with the action contraption," because it helps to develop a small child's co-ordination and architectural skills. Kids love it because it's a battle for survival. Mice the world over remained unimpressed.

SPACE HOPPERS

Mettoy
1971—Present day

Italian inventor Aquilino Cosani had been making gymnastic balls since 1963 when he invented the "Pon Pon." Cosani redesigned and improved the jumping ball—he made it into a heavy rubber balloon about 22" in diameter, with two rubber handles protruding from the top. A valve at the top allowed the balloon to be inflated by a bicycle pump or car-tyre pump. He called it HOP and patented the idea in Italy in 1968, and in the United States in 1971. However, the name Space Hopper was never registered.

Hence Mettoy's Space Hopper with horns instead of handle, and bizarre animal face.

CONNECT 4

Milton Bradley
1974—Present Day

Known variously as Plot Four, Four in a Row or Four in a Line, this vertical strategy game has been around in various guises for hundreds of years. It picked up its most common colloquial name, though, during the time Captain James Cook took it away in his voyages. Cook was known for passing away the endless hours at sea playing the game, so much so that it became known as "Captain's Mistress."

In 1974, the game reached a new audience when Milton Bradley renamed it Connect 4. Its simplicity made it perfect for any technological advances and in the 1980s and 1990s it got further leases of life through GameBoy and the internet.

RUBIK'S CUBE

Ideal Toys
1979—Present day

The biggest fad of the 1980s was invented in 1974 by Ernö Rubik, a Hungarian obsessed with 3D geometry who was inspired by pebbles on the shore of the River Danube, where he began visualizing his 3D cube.

For almost three years it remained a craze purely among Rubik's friends and students for whom he created Cubes, but by early 1978, demand for this strange toy began to grow. In 1979, after the Nurenberg toy show, the Ideal Toy Company brought it to the mass market although—and maybe uniquely for a toy—it needed the help of mathematician David Singmaster and a front cover of *Scientific American* magazine to raise its profile.

SILLY PUTTY

Arnold Clark/Barney-Smith
1950—Present day

From the strangest origins the strangest things occur. Chemical engineer James Wright discovered that when mixed, boric acid and silicon oil made a synthetic goo which bounced, stretched, withstood decay and had the ability to lift images off the printed page. It came to the attention of a toy shop owner who offered an ounce in a clear plastic case for sale at $2. It was shown at the 1950 New York Toy Fair. Marketing consultant Peter Hodgson took up the goo's cause and believed in it enough to turn it into a best-selling toy. In 1957, after being endorsed on the *Howdy Doody Show*, Silly Putty became an official toy fad.

By the 1960s, it was becoming popular worldwide and was sold in Russia and Europe. It even went to the moon with Apollo 8. In 1977 the Barney-Smith company bought the rights to Silly Putty and it continues to be a top toy.

TOP TRUMPS

Parker Brothers
1974—Present day

Once upon a time, Top Trumps was called War and it was a regular card game focusing on the highest value of the card. Parker Brothers/Hasbro licensed it from Winning Moves in Europe and turned it into the most popular card series ever. Initially there were six games, each containing 30 cards packaged in a flip-top carrying case for two or more players. Each was available with a different theme. Where War was simply about the highest value of the card though, the joy of Top Trumps is in the nerdy collection and trading of statistics.

The most geeky set is Ultimate Military Jets, in which cards detail maximum speed, maximum height, range, maximum takeoff weight and wing span.

PLAY-DOH

Kenner/Hasbro
1957–Present day

Like many simple ideas, Play-Doh had simple beginnings. Joe McVicker worked for a detergent company and when his teacher sister-in-law came home one day and said that the modeling clay at her school was too hard for the kids to use, Joe got to thinking. What about that soft, putty-like stuff he used to clean wallpaper?

Joe was a millionaire by the time he was 27. Play-Doh was originally available in one color (off white) and one size (1½ pound can), before the more famous three-can yellow, red, and blue pack hit the market in 1957. Play-Doh Compound celebrated its 40th birthday by introducing two more colors, Gold and Silver, fun scents and a soap, Splash "n" Play-Doh. It even joined the techno world with a CD-ROM game, Play-Doh Creations, an educational software program for children.

STRATEGO

Milton Bradley
1961–Present Day

Patented by Milton Bradley in 1960, Stratego hit the market in 1961. A game of skill and strategy, there's a battlefield on which each player commands an army of 40 pieces. Pieces are only marked on one side, and you have to remember your opponents' actions throughout the game. If it is not completed within an hour and a quarter, it's a draw. It bears some resemblance to the low-tech Battleships game.

Stratego has a huge following in Europe and there's an extensive tournament circuit in Germany and Holland. A ten-round Swiss tournament takes place four times a year. The winners from each qualify for the grand finals at the end of the year.

SPIROGRAPH

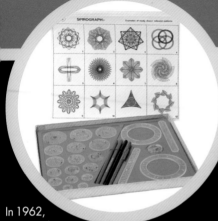

invention at the 1965 Nuremberg International Toy Fair, where execs from Kenner bought the U.S. rights. Kenner was optimistic, but even they didn't expect sales of 5.5 million in the first two years. It was also voted the best educational toy four years in a row (1966 to 1969).

The fantastic thing about Spirograph was that you couldn't do it wrong. It made perfect results every time. If you held everything down, you couldn't go wrong. Well you could because the little pins that had to hold the outer wheel down were woeful, but that apart it was foolproof.

In 1962, Denys Fisher was designing bomb detonators for NATO, when his research inspired him to invent the spirograph. The Fishers first showed their

MONOPOLY

Former heating engineer Charles Darrow's world had been turned upside down by the stock market crash of 1929. In 1930, he found himself on holiday in Atlantic City and started on an idea he'd had. Soon, Darrow had made a prototype of a new board game and began selling them. He tried to sell the idea to Parker Brothers, the big games company, who rejected it. Driven by word-of-mouth recommendation, however, Darrow's sales continued to grow until Christmas 1934 when, coincidentally, the daughter of the president of Parker Brothers bought a set.

Parkers bought the game outright, and Darrow received a royalty on every game sold.

KERPLUNK

Ideal/Mattel
1967–Present day

Like Buckaroo and Mousetrap (see page 117), Kerplunk was one of those games which used as many plastic bits as possible, thus ensuring that they were unplayable after three days because bits would invariably go missing.

Ideal first released Kerplunk in 1967. In the box was a clear plastic tube, 30 thin sticks, and 32 marbles. The sticks acted as a web that held the marbles at the top of the tube. The idea was, like all the best ideas, really very simple: to get as many sticks out without letting any of the marbles fall through. It needed a steady hand of course, as you slowly (or quickly) removed the sticks from the marble-filled tube until the whole thing goes Ker, and then Plunk. You can now buy electronic versions.

DON'T SPILL THE BEANS

Schaper/Milton Bradley
1965–Present day

Two to four young children drop beans onto the pot's lid, one by one. The more beans there are, the more care they must take. If (when) they upset the balance of the pot, they spill the beans. Then everyone squeals and has a good time. It came with a stand, pot, four bean bowls, a bean bag, and real red beans.

Schaper made some of the most intriguing games of the Baby Boomer era, and are best known for favorites like Ants In The Pants, Don't Break The Ice, and this. Most were based on players taking turns until some catastrophic event befell the unfortunate loser. Another favourite was The Voodoo Doll game, where took turns poking the voodoo doll with needles until the loser poked the booby-trapped hole and the witch doctor burst out of his hut.

Metal toy soldiers had been around for centuries, but they were by nature expensive. However, this all changed in the 1950s when a revolutionary new material called "plastic" became freely available. The advent of injection moulding made it possible to produce toy soldiers at a fraction of what they'd previously cost. That was the green light for designers who saw the potential to not only make soldiers but also accessories, so a kid could get all he needed in one Playset to re-create history on his living room floor. And no-one took advantage of this new development like Louis Marx and the Marx Toy Company.

The combination of dynamically sculpted figures in action poses, with accessories, metal buildings, and tie-ins to movies and television shows, captured the imagination of millions of baby-boomer boys. Typically, a set consisted of several pieces of lithographed tin that could be assembled into structures including a ranch cabin, a service station, a fort, an Old West street and an air base. Each set also had an array of plastic figures appropriate to the theme: cowboys and Indians, soldiers, farm animals, and so on.

Cleverly, Marx recycled the original templates of his figures to reflect the TV hits of the day, turning a once popular movie hero into a new star of the smaller screen by smelting and remodeling.

Marx Playsets evolved through the 1950s and peaked in terms of elaborateness in the 1960s. Their popularity declined in the following decade as *Star Wars* conquered the Boys' Toys market.

ANT FARMS

Uncle Milton
1956—Present day

One day in 1956 Milton Levine, who'd made a name for himself selling mail-order novelty toys, placing adverts in comics for "a hundred cowboys and Indians for only a buck," was sitting by a pool watching a group of ants go about their business. Then he drifted off, dreaming of the time when he was a kid and kept ants in a jar. He used to watch them dig and work and... Eureka!

He sat down and designed how it would work—it had to be a bit more interesting than just some ants in a jar—and before long, he'd dubbed himself Uncle Milton and called his new project an Ant Farm.

The transparent, sand-filled Ant Farm package allowed you to observe the inscrutable doings of a colony of harvester ants. It was, as Uncle Milton said, "a lesson in nature study." The adverts said: "Watch them dig tunnels! See them build rooms! Marvel as they erect bridges and move mountains before your very eyes! The Ant Farm is a living TV screen that will keep you interested for hours!" They sold for $1.98 and, during the next two decades, Levine sold over 12 million of them.

The kit included a break-resistant escape-proof habitat (9 x 6"), four Antports with tubing for connecting to other Ant Farms, clean tunneling sand, an illustrated *Ant Watcher's Manual*, and tip-proof stand. The ants were ordered separately.

Kids could watch their ants build nests, look for food, look after

A MESS OF ANTS

Ant colony life has evolved over the past 100 million years. So much is unknown of these complex, diverse social insects, yet they make up a large part of the animal biomass on the planet. Some scientists think that 30% of the animal biomass of the Amazon Basin is made up of ants, that 10% of the animal biomass of the world is ants, and that a further 10% is Termites. This means that "social insects" could make up an incredible 20% of the total animal biomass of the planet.

NO BOYS ALLOWED

The ants used were red ants—harvester ants—from the Californian desert. They are one of the few of the world's 9,000 species of ant that work during daylight and were big enough (a quarter of an inch) to see but too big to escape through the air holes. Only the females were used because the males don't respond well to captivity. Naturally.

The Ant Farm awaits inhabitants

the young, care for the old… If you were lucky they might even fight. Ants can be extremely devious, using propaganda, surveillance, and assault singly or in combination to overcome their enemies. They can drop stones on their enemies and even take hostages back to their colonies as slaves. They cannot, however, put a group of humans in a box and sell it to their kids.

At $2.98, the Ant Farm was an instant hit. The line, which has sold more than 20 million units over the years, eventually expanded into six versions, including a "giant" model aimed at schoolrooms, kits of interlocking ant farm modules and even the Xtreme Ant Farm, equipped with a tiny rock-climbing wall.

Critics of the Ant Farm (and there were some) complained that because there was no Queen—government regulations wouldn't allow it—it was an inauthentic environment. Did the kids who owned an Ant Farm care?

You can still buy the original Ant Farm, as well as numerous variations on it.

INDEX

Credits

Page	Property	Registered Trademark Owner
10	GI Joe	Hasbro, Inc.
12	Action Man	Hasbro, Inc.
14	Captain Action	Playing Mantis, Inc.
19	Sea Devils	Thomas Lowe Ventures, Inc.
21	Captain America	Marvel Entertainment Group
24	James Bond 007	Danjaq SA
25	Corgi	Mettoy Co Ltd
26	6 Million Dollar Man	Universal City Studios, Inc.
27	Starsky & Hutch	Columbia Pictures Industries, Inc.
28	Lone Ranger	Classic Media, Inc.
29	Incredible Hulk	Marvel Characters, Inc.
29	Wonder Woman	DC Comics, Inc.
30	Dinky Toys	J Lloyd International
30	Space 1999	ITC Entertainment Group Limited
31	Thunderbirds	ITC Entertainment Group Limited
33	Captain Scarlet	Carlton International Media Limited
36	Star Wars	Lucasfilm Licensing Ltd
38	Star Trek	Paramount Pictures Corporation
39	Buck Rogers	Trustees of the Dille Family Trust
40	Doctor Who	British Broadcasting Corporation
41	Lost in Space	Red Skelton Productions, Inc.
42	Zeroids	Thomas Lowe Ventures, Inc.
43	Robby the Robot	Turner Entertainment Co.
50	Major Matt Mason	Mattel, Inc.
50	Capt. Lazer	Mattel, Inc.
51	Sgt. Storm	Mattel, Inc.
52	Colorforms	University Games Corporation
53	Godzilla	Toho Co Ltd
56	Evel Knievel	Knievel, Robert Craig
58	Beatles	Apple Corps, Ltd
59	Monkees	Columbia Pictures Industries, Inc.
62	Matchbox	Mattel, Inc.
64	Hot Wheels	Mattel, Inc.
66	Scalextric	Hornby Hobbies Limited
70	Johnny Lightning	Thomas Lowe Ventures, Inc.
71	Tootsietoys	Processed Plastic Company
72	Tonka Toys	Hasbro, Inc.
73	Siku	Sieper-Werke GmbH
73	Majorette	Societe Nouvelle Majorette
74	Knight Rider	Universal City Studios, Inc.
74	Kojak	Universal City Studios, Inc.
75	Dukes of Hazard	Warner Bros. Entertainment Inc.
75	The Saint	ITC Entertainment Holdings, Ltd.
78	Lionel Trains	Lionel L.L.C.
80	American Flyer	Lionel, L.L.C
81	Tyco	Tyco Industries, Inc.
82	Revell	Revell, Inc.
83	Hornby	Hornby Hobbies Limited
85	Atlas	Atlas Model Railroad Company, Inc.
88	Airfix	Humbrol Limited
89	Kenner	CPG Products Corporation
95	Nu Craft	Paul K. Guillow, Inc
96	Remco	JAKKS Pacific, Inc.
100	Erector	Meccano S.A.
101	Meccano	Meccano S.A.
103	View-Master	Tyco Industries, Inc.
104	Lego	Kirkbi AG
108	Atari	Atrari Interactive. Inc.
109	Apple	Apple Computer, Inc.
110	Commodore	Commodore International B.V.
111	Tandy	Corporation d.b.a. Radio Shack
112	Pong	Atrari Interactive. Inc.
113	Space Invaders	Taito America Corporation
116	Slinky	Poof-Slinky, Inc.
116	Etch a Sketch	Ohio Art Company, Inc.
117	Mouse trap	Hasbro, Inc.
118	Connect Four	Hasbro, Inc.
118	Rubik's Cube	Seven Town's Ltd.
119	Silly Putty	Binney & Smith, Inc.
119	Top Trumps	Winning Moves International Ltd
120	Play Doh	Hasbro, Inc.
120	Stratego	Hausemann & Hotte B.V.
121	Spirograph	Tonka Corporation
121	Monopoly	Tonka Corporation
122	Kerplunk	Ideal Toy Corporation, Inc.
122	Don't Spill the Beans	Hasbro, Inc.
124	Ant Farm	Uncle Milton Industries, Inc.

Acknowledgements

The author would like to thank the following for their assistance in the making of this book: Darryl Dupuis of www.robotnut.com, John Michlig of Fully Articulated Productions, Patrick Karris (aka the Robothunter), John Rigg, Maryann Sell, Steve Dixon (www.mysite4u.com), David Pierce (of www.frontier-history.com), Joe Sikora, Tony Stanford, Derek Whitman, Jamie Cogan (of www.astromodels.uk.com), Dave Mamer at Big Island Toys, Justin Pinchot (of www.toyraygun.com), all at Toyzine, Tom Heaton of Vintage Toy Room, all at www.gogomag.com, Joyce Grant at Time Warp Toys, the Train Collectors Association, and Dr Toy.

Special thanks to Jay H. Miller for assistance with Erector Sets on page 100 and to Joe Siepietoski for Hubley on page 90.